Age and the Antique Sideboard

Barbara Spencer

Illustrations by Katie Beltrami

Matador
9 Priory Business Park,
Wistow Road, Kibworth Beauchamp,
Leicestershire. LE8 0RX
Tel: 0116 279 2299
Email: books@troubador.co.uk
Web: www.troubador.co.uk/matador
Twitter: @matadorbooks

ISBN 978 1788032 810

British Library Cataloguing in Publication Data.
A catalogue record for this book is available from the British Library.

Printed and bound in the UK by TJ International, Padstow, Cornwall
Typeset in 12pt Bembo by Troubador Publishing Ltd, Leicester, UK

Matador is an imprint of Troubador Publishing Ltd

This book is dedicated to my long-suffering family, especially my daughter and granddaughter, Aletia

Barbara Spencer

"You are old, Father William," the young man said,
"And your hair has become very white;
And yet you incessantly stand on your head—
Do you think, at your age, it is right?"

"In my youth," Father William replied to his son,
"I feared it might injure the brain;
But now that I'm perfectly sure I have none,
Why, I do it again and again."

Age and the Antique Sideboard

Barbara Spencer

My love affair with both life and words began in 1969, when 'Fashion' Magazine paid me the goodly sum of £25 to write an article about travel. Other articles followed and from these humble beginnings came children's books, full of rib-tickling humour and scintillating action.

However, my desire to wax lyrical about the absurdity of life remained and whilst journeying by train to some far distant school or to a signing at Waterstones, I began scribbling down my thoughts. Blogs, anecdotes and short stories followed. Now of an age to remember the past, I thought, why not? There has to be heaps of people around like me … well, not exactly like me but near enough to enjoy and remember how life once was.

Contents

A journey of a thousand miles begins with a single step

It is better to travel hopefully than to arrive

A picture paints a thousand words

Appearances can be deceptive

All that glitters is not gold

Distance lends enchantment to the view

All good things comes to he who waits

*A journey of a thousand miles
begins with a single step*

A spot of trouble in my waterworks

So there I am sitting on the floor with my head under the sink.

The question: **what am I doing there?** is the wrong question. The answer is plainly obvious, since I am surrounded by the bowels of plumbing: two outlet pipes and a u-bend.

The question: **what am I doing there at eleven o'clock at night?** is also the wrong question. And, had it been asked at the time, I would have said, it is also somewhat irritating. It is quite obvious what I am doing: I am cleaning the drain.

However, the question: do you know how to fit these pieces back together again? That question — however hurtful in its tendency to cast aspersions on my mechanical ability — *is* entirely relevant to the problem in hand. Bulls-eye!

You could then continue and ask: But shouldn't you be in bed? Or: **Won't you get cramp sitting on the floor like that?**

However relevant such questions might be when you are in a tight spot (as I was, crouched on my side with my head jammed inside the cupboard under the sink), such perception, however kindly meant, does nothing to resolve the jigsaw puzzle in my lap. And however much I lecture myself that I have done this before (several times) and have profited by having clean smelling drains for yet another six months, the pieces fail to gel: for I simply cannot remember.

Was the u-bend under this drain or indeed under that?

Have I lost a piece?

I rush outside and examine the spot on the ground, where I had tipped the disgustingly gruesome water. No! There are no misplaced pieces of pipe ... only an inquisitive cat.

So if it is all here in my lap, why does this pipe have three outlets? I'm positive it had only two before I washed it. I scrutinise the pieces. Honest, there really are only two bits of pipe into which it can fit.

So how come I also have three washers left over?

And where the hell did I hang my rubber gloves?

Visualisation of the drainage system fails to produce an image of the piece of pipe on which my rubber gloves have, in fact, hung for the past five years. Instead, it produces cramp, my toes curling up like slices of stale bread, causing me to screech in agony and hang on to my toes until the spasm has passed.

I glance at my watch. One o'clock! I look outside at the peaceful square, neighbours on all sides sleeping soundly, the square cocooned in a haven of blissful quiet.

Nothing for it but to give in. And yet …

'Tomorrow,' I say aloud, my tone as sorrowful as a solitary nighthawk over Kurdistan, 'the moment I awake I will call the plumber and that will cost me at least a hundred pounds.'

It is amazing how the threat of unwanted expenditure clarifies the aging mind.

Instantly the pieces make sense, the long white tubes clipping neatly together to form two drains, one horizontal bar (on which my rubber gloves hang), and a u-bend, each piece clean and sweet-smelling and designed to carry, without leaking, waste water into the municipal drain.

One last job to be done: I stick my head back under the sink, working my way along each pipe inch by inch, trying to memorise where each piece lives in relation to the next.

'Well' I say, glancing at my watch and a silently sleeping square. 'At least I've saved myself a ton of money.'

And on that happy thought I take myself off to bed.

Dads, Daffodils and Victoriana

Wordsworth wrote odes to daffodils. If I wrote poetry, I'd write about young dads strolling down the street with babies or little children clutching their hand or astride their shoulders, the joy of fatherhood writ loud on Dad's face.

For me it is the most uplifting of sights and one that encourages hope for the future. My childhood with a father, who happened to be a leftover from Victoriana, like the fabled aspidistra, was all dusty and spiky.

Okay, blame the Queen and not the man, who in her black bombazine encouraged women throughout her realm to follow the adage, *spare the rod and spoil the child*. As a result of his upbringing, my father did not approve of men or, more particularly, men who came calling on his daughters.

On one occasion my older sister brought home her beau. At work all day, he asked if he might wash and shave before heading with her out to a dance. Unfortunately, all he had brought with him was a new-fangled electric razor and, even more unfortunately, the only socket it fitted was in my parents' bedroom.

With father due home any minute, the event went down like this:

Young man in vest shaving, razor plugged into wall lamp socket.

Mother with bedroom window wide open, craning out to catch sight of car as it turned into the road.

Me sitting on stairs by front door, in case father made it through the front door without being spotted.

Sister, whose boyfriend he was, having hysterics in her bedroom.

On another occasion, she and I were playing tennis with two boys from down the road and had, somewhat foolishly, brought them into the house for a refreshing drink. When the key sounded in the front door, I tore out into the hall instructed to create a diversion and pacify the enemy or fall on my sword.

On that occasion my even-older sister had phoned. Hastily reporting and telling Father, 'it's really, really urgent, you ring back,' I waited, breath held. A satisfactory outcome to the telephone call gave me courage enough to come out with the immortal words, *'Father, we have been playing tennis with some boys from down the road.'*

I opened the sitting room door to find the room empty, the culprits having left by the window.

A brave new world

Once upon a time I possessed a very nice and very cheap mobile phone. It cost £10. And, yes, maybe I did carry it about for two years before learning how to text. But I did learn … at least enough to text my granddaughter, to inform her I was parked outside the school gates. And, yes, maybe it did spend most of the time switched off so I missed alerts from Orange and an occasional 'missed call' from my granddaughter … but it worked. And it was there in an emergency, which is what I needed.

Then one night I saw my daughter's phone.

With the consummate ease of an Olympic gymnast, she flipped through photographs, maps, books, more photographs, train timetables … and it was big and luxurious looking, and as drool-worthy as chocolate cake.

And so I entered the world of modernity and bought a really, really, proper phone – you know the type you have to recharge every night and it already has a Google App installed that tells you where to go and takes a picture of it.

A tutorial from my daughter and I am away.

Next day, a second tutorial from my daughter.

Unfortunately, this time I am not wearing my glasses, so haven't a clue what she is on about when she points to a blue blob on the screen and announces this is where I live.

This is followed next day by a tutorial from my granddaughter.

She introduces me to QWERTY and would kill for a phone like mine. To show me how to use it, she snatches it away, presses keys at the speed of light, says, *'there you are'* and hands the phone back, leaving me none the wiser.

A week later and I am asking myself why did I bother. I really was quite content to take a book in my handbag, read a map, and charge the battery on my old phone every three weeks or so.

Man's Ingenuity: A conundrum

Today's must have gadgets: Tablets, Ipads, E-readers, the now – almost extinct – mp3 player, mobile phones, play stations and games, Facebook, Twitter, Farmville, Minecraft – the list is endless – are quietly and insidiously eroding original thought from this generation, and replacing it with an ability to follow a sequence of instructions and the skill needed to push buttons, faster and faster.

The problem I have with this phenomenon is that these fiendish devices, which are busily rewiring our brains and turning the next generation of children into zombies, are created by the most original thinkers and forward-looking people on the planet.

They don't make them like they used to

'Who?'

'Singers,' I say to my granddaughter.

'Singers who?' (Note the exquisite terminology.)

'People like Joan Sutherland. She could fill Lincoln Centre in New York with the most glorious sound – as clear at the back of the upper circle as it was in the stalls. No mikes, no tricks, no gimmicks.'

'What's your point?'

'Have you listened to entrants on X Factor, who tootle away or howl into a microphone only to be told they have a wonderful voice?'

13

'Yes, and it's cool.'

'Screaming a melody into a microphone whilst bending ones knees can NOT be described as cool,' I pontificate. 'Nor is it a description of a singer with a brilliant voice. Do you know that real singers spend years learning their trade before casting themselves onto the world stage? I mean how many of that lot ever think of taking lessons, learning how to breathe properly and project their voice.'

'You like X-Factor.'

'Well, yes, but that's not the point.'

'That is the exactly the point, Baba. X-Factor's entertainment, a bit of fun; it's not meant to be taken seriously. Besides, there are some great singers. What about Adele?'

'Oh, yes, I forgot her.'

(Joan Sutherland, who died 11th October 2010, rose to fame at Covent Garden in Lucia de Lammermoor in 1959. Living in New York in the seventies, my evenings were mostly spent queuing for tickets to the Metropolitan Opera in Lincoln Centre, where I was lucky enough to see her playing opposite Luciano Pavarotti, with whom she recorded several of her most famous roles.)

The preposition that became a verb

I failed my English Grammar 'O' level first time round, retaking it in the November, and I still can't cope with commas. And if someone starts nattering on about dependent clauses, I shut down. Yet, even I know the word *of* is not a verb.

You cannot say, 'I should of gone to the shops today.' Maybe you should have gone to the shops today, particularly if your fridge is empty but not of ... never of.

So why has it entered common parlance? (Everyday speech to you and me.)

And where has the H-aitch in aitch come from?

The Oxford dictionary states that the 8th letter of the alphabet is aitch. And in pronouncing the word you do not aspirate the first letter which is aitch. The aitch in aitch is pronounced aitch!

Got it!

It's always been aitch and always will be aitch, I want to yell from the highest mountain.

(Heavens, we could really go the distance with this aitch-stuff, exactly like a bantam-weight amateur boxer going three rounds at the Olympics.)

I mean, if you are determined to mispronounce aitch, why not make a real meal of it and pronounce ef ... ffffffffffff ... the noise a sewing machine makes. And what about em ... mmmmmmmmmmmm ... like a motor mower in need of petrol.

And while I am having a grumble, where did MYSELF come from? Myself and my husband and children. Whatever happened to: My husband and I?

Or do we now think we are more important than anyone else, including our husband and children?

Life's like that

It is all so unreasonable – this getting up at seven full of good intentions. You'd think by the time you reach maturity + ten or twenty more years, you'd be wise to the fact that good intentions resemble the old saying: *rain before seven, fine before eleven.*

Except with good intentions it's the other way round – by eleven they're gone, vanished in a puff of smoke. Rather like the genie after Aladdin had made his three wishes. So today, swimming didn't happen, nor the ironing, nor the housework, nor the car cleaning. Worse the few thousand words I meant to write – not so much as a scribble.

Ah, well, there's always tomorrow. Meanwhile, the characters in my next book are stranded in a wood – I simply haven't written them out of it yet.

How much longer, I hear them cry?

Tomorrow – maybe!

Boats, Bungalows and B & B's

Cornwall is unlike any other county in the UK and the only one to which I will never return. In fact my strength of feeling is so er ... er ... strong, I am about to pen a letter to the County Council suggesting that before next summer they install electronic signboards on the A30 and A38, at their crossing point into Cornwall.

'Why?' I hear you ask.

Out of consideration for visitors.

Imagine their gratitude if, before embarking on the final sixty miles, they were forewarned about parking:

Perrenporth Beach – 2 spaces

Truro – good possibility

Mevagissy – no chance

or even

Cornwall – full to bursting – try again next year.

**CORNWALL FULL
TRY LATER**

Besides which, it might just avert a bloodbath between motorists struggling to get into the same parking place, egged on by precocious children and an irritable wife, fed-up with spending two hours stuck in traffic.

Meanwhile, spare a thought for the poor residents. For them summers have to be pure unadulterated hell.

Which brings me to the English institution of Bed and Breakfast. I vaguely remember during a family holiday shortly after the war, my mother complaining most bitterly about the boarding house in Deal, where the landlady, despite having our food coupons for the week, had served up cornflakes with watered-down milk.

I am not stating that B&B's have not progressed in sixty years, I am only saying, my recent experience leads me to wonder if they have.

First there was the parking.

On the side of a cliff, where no council official in their right mind would possibly have considered granting a licence for a ten room B&B with only five parking spaces; meaning, you either curtailed your day's activities returning early to grab a parking space or wandered back and forth all night like a wailing banshee.

Then there were the fire doors.

The one at the top of the main staircase actually sat on the top step, and since its spring was designed to increase the pulling-power of a weight lifter, this proved quite a challenge. Once open, you held it open with your bottom long enough to negotiate the first step. Otherwise, the door slammed into your back with such force you broke the eighty-yard indoor sprint record on the way down.

Then there were the bedroom doors.

All new, they should have been fitted with a can of WD40 taped to the door handle. As you pushed down the handle, excruciating squeaks, rather like a pig being slaughtered, emanated from the hinge, while the key turning in the lock, mimicked the sound-effects of a Hammer Horror Film.

Tragically, I belong to the fraternity that has to get up at night to go to the loo. The cacophony of sounds, which accompanied my nervous journey to the bathroom, was of the ilk to encourage some ambitious teenager, had he heard them, into starting a new pop group.

SCREECH-CLATTER went my lock, SQUEAK my bedroom door opened, BANG it shut. (My poor neighbour, who had been snoring peacefully, awoke with a start as the thin partition wall vibrated.)

(How do I know this? I heard him click on the light!)

˙THUD said the fire-door, through which I had to pass on my way to the bathroom, despite an inch by inch effort to close it softly, CREAK went the bathroom door, CLICK-BUZZ the pull-light cord resonated as with a WHIRRING noise the extractor fan started up.

Mouse-like, I CLICKED, CREAKED, THUDDED, BANGED and SQUEAKED my way back to my bedroom.

(Have I mentioned turning the key in the lock?)

Terrified I might need the loo again, I lay awake. And guess what …?

Still, I dare not get up. No way could I face that again. Doubtless, twice in one night would herald a lynch mob outside my door at dawn waiting for me to emerge. Crossing my legs, I forced myself to endure and stay in bed, too timid to run the assault course again – even if I had paid handsomely for the room.

Then there was breakfast.

With neatly set-up tables in straight lines, every so often the door creaked open to admit a series of couples, who hovered awkwardly at the entrance hoping a waitress

21

would appear and direct them to a table, not already *bagged* by the couple who had arrived two or three days before. Once seated, they began a conversation in stilted whispers all about stuff they would never dream of talking about at home – such as Aunty Bessie going into hospital for a hip replacement.

The waitress appeared asking *tea or coffee* before handing me an elaborate, leather-bound menu extolling the virtues of the extensive and traditional English breakfast, including brown and white toast, and several varieties of egg.

'Do you have any fruit?'

'Fruit? I don't think so.'

The second day, I perused the leather-bound volume more thoroughly, and discovered the magical word *yoghurt* tucked away under *All-bran*. It was as if the landlady was saying, somewhat apologetically: I have to offer it, you know, some people like it.

Okay, so the views are wonderful. Magical even. But once you've seen them, you've seen them. Next time I consider taking a holiday in England, I shall inform all and sundry I will be away for the week, stock up on fresh coffee and croissant, luxurious strawberry jam and peaches, draw the curtains and spend my days looking at all my old holiday snaps – full of wonderful views ...

And have a great time.

Going Bananas

Did you know fishing is the most popular sport in Britain? I didn't. When I did think about it, I found myself speculating as to whether an activity which consists of catching a fish and throwing it back in again, can ever be called sporting.

Be that as it may; according to officialdom fishing is still more popular than golf. Although, if you really come to think about it, chasing a white ball for five miles is pretty silly too!

Nevertheless, I am convinced that statistics will support the statement that golfers consume more bananas than any other sporting group.

Golfers, the length and breadth of Britain, have discovered the magical properties of slow-release carbohydrates which sustain them until they hole out on the 18th, while the skins, nonchalantly flicked into the bushes, provide food for birds or compost for the ground.

Among golfers, therefore, the commonplace banana has acquired an almost *mystical* reputation.

'Would you like a banana? I've brought two,' will follow a particularly nasty slice on the 10th, which lands your ball in the woods, and your partner trying to conceal his/her irritation.

And missing a 6ft putt on the 4th will initiate immediate consumption of a banana, since you are totally convinced that its healing powers will remedy your tendency to pull your putts. In which case, a similar distance on the 5th green will prove no problem.

It comes as no surprise, therefore, when faced with playing an Open on an unknown course in Cornwall, I decided to buy some bananas. At that point, little did I realise my search would take me the length and breadth of the county, before arriving at the inescapable conclusion that bananas have never been heard of south of Devon.

'Bananas!'

The reaction which greeted my polite enquiry was similar to that of a greengrocer in the Second World War, whose shop contained one orange.

Having discovered that the words, 'Country Store', which in Somerset heralds a roadside fruit and veg stand selling punnets of strawberries and raspberries, related to corrugated sheds spewing out paving stones and lengths of wood (believe me I visited five), I decided to check out all the villages along the A392. Someone, somewhere, has to sell bananas.

Cornwall is to be complimented on the quality of its 'A' roads. Superbly maintained, they unfailingly indicate the whereabouts of a tourist attraction or village. Unfortunately, once off the highway you plunge into cavernous single-track lanes, guarded by tall hedges. And it is only when you come across a signpost to yet another village that you realise you have already passed the one you were seeking … it was those half-dozen houses you passed a while back with a pub, but no shop selling bananas.

Bloody-mindedly I fought on, politely pulling into narrow passing zones to allow oncoming traffic to proceed, from time to time catching an elusive gleam of water through dense hedgerows, becoming more and more convinced that I would stumble across a mysterious Frenchman aboard his yacht, *The Seagull,* in some watery creek.

Finally, I gave up and returned to the main road.

Exhausted, I drove back to St Austell, eventually passing through a proper village, which boasted a sub-post office selling comestibles but no bananas. Surely, there has to be a vegetable shop on the periphery of St Austell? There wasn't or if there was, I didn't see it.

In sombre mood I set off for the golf course – banana-less …

… and had a most disgusting round.

I did eventually discover a Tesco who, as everyone knows, sells bananas, although that was not until I was heading back to Somerset at the end of this 'never to be forgotten' day, the responsibility for which I lay entirely on my lack of bananas. The store in question lay on the far side of St. Austell on the A392 heading towards Liskeard, which was a fat lot of use.

Do you remember our alarmist cry when supermarkets first appeared: 'You mark my words, small shops will die out?'

They have!

At least the ones selling bananas have.

The Machiavellian plot of Tesco, Sainsbury and the like, is almost complete. The only thing left to be done is for town planners to include a supermarket logo on all road signs: A392, Liskeard, Plymouth and Tesco Superstore. Otherwise golfers will never be able to find bananas in a strange town.

*It is better to travel hopefully
than to arrive*

~∞~

Embarking on a tour of England

I know very little about England. The country of my birth, as a child I was taken on 'educational visits'. In my father's language this meant either the golf club or trolling the backstreets of Birmingham, where barefooted children sat patiently outside a public house waiting for mum or dad to emerge; the idea being that I should be grateful for what I had got. A little later, if I was especially fortunate, I was taken on a trip to my father's industrial mecca, Sheffield, where black belching chimneys poked into the sky guarded by glass-strewn brick walls, and iron-clad gates hinted at the presence of yet another colossus of steel.

Not surprisingly, living away from England for so many years, in my mind these places have remained the same.

More recently, visiting branches of Waterstones for a Saturday signing has served as an introduction to towns and cities never before visited, leaving me stunned by both change and progress. Smart, litter-free streets, bright colours … and no factories belching smoke.

Yet, in some ways, very little'has changed. Battling

my way around Bristol the other day constantly asking directions, it struck me that Brits are pretty much as they have always been – courteous, helpful and polite.

Except for teenagers! Bewilderment is their overriding emotion if questioned about a street name located more than one hundred yards distant.

Dug Up

"Oh! Mr Porter, what shall I do?
I want to go to Birmingham
And they're taking me on to Crewe …"

The words of the old song reverberate through my head whenever I think of *England* and *travelling* in the same sentence. Monsters feature somewhere too because England can become a hugely ungainly beast when you need to circumnavigate it. (Anyone attempted the M25 recently?)

Sadly, in the south-west we are still suffering the consequences of Dr Beeching who closed our railway lines. With early-morning traffic stretching like the arms of a multi-tasking octopus, frustrated drivers leave home earlier and earlier in an attempt to reach their place of work before the knell of doom strikes. *(Tut, tut. Late again, Mr Brown?)*

A while back, heading for Bristol for an interview at the BBC in Whiteladies Road, I almost ran out of petrol standing still. (Hasn't anyone heard of global warming?)

Distances multiply; days come and go, as you crawl along at zero miles per hour. Returning home, after a long drive and an even longer day signing books, tired and anxious to put my feet up, I have been brainwashed into obeying every one of an unremitting series of speed-restriction signs that pre-empt a minute cluster of cottages, and which add at least thirty minutes to my journey.

For those of us living in rural Somerset, the question that balances most uneasily on our lips when contemplating a long journey is: do I drive twenty-seven miles to the nearest motorway or use the shorter route across country?

Rumours abound that this is destined to become a specialist subject on Mastermind.

Drive across country?

In summer?

Pass!

Once, heading across country proved a fillip to the soul, an enjoyable adventure, gazing at scenery little changed from when the Normans and Saxons walked across it. These days, it is simply a disagreeable alternative to driving in convoy along a motorway. With gay abandon, CCs (county councils to you and me) close roads for weeks on end. Not for them consideration of the already hard-done-by motorist, with night-work outlawed, and day work too, come to think of it. (I mean, how often do you see men working on a hole in the road?) Instead, CCs unhesitatingly divert already frothing-at-the-mouth and hair-tearing drivers miles in the opposite direction.

No doubt, by the time I have carried out a few more events, I will be putting my house up for sale and moving to a town where there is a railway station.

Note to self: Send memo urging drivers to use extreme caution when approaching either Radstock or Coxley in Somerset and to have an escape route plotted in case things go badly.

'Go badly? What on earth do you mean?'

I mean these two locations are among the top ten venues in the country for being dug up. Do councils have a grudge against the people who live there? Perhaps when deciding which roads to dig up next, they pass a hat round the council chamber filled with lots of bits of paper and only two names.

'Oh, look, it's Radstock. Aren't they lucky.'

I drove through Radstock earlier today and spotted a yellow notice announcing a ten-week closure for drains.

How inconsiderate. You'd think they might have waited until the fresh tarmac laid yesterday had settled.

Manners maketh man

The biggest difference between good teachers and the not-so good, and one that socks you on the jaw every time you encounter it, is not a lack of educational ability but an absence of social grace. I mean, you would think if you found a stranger lolling about your staffroom a few questions might just pop into your head, such as: could this person be a terrorist, a paedophile or perhaps even a poltergeist? At the very least ... What the hell is this strange person doing drinking our coffee and eating our biscuits? We have to pay for those.

A frequent visitor to both primary and secondary schools, I have discovered etiquette to be a relatively unknown quality in staff rooms. I deliver my lecture to a year group and head into the staffroom for coffee or lunch, and staff walk and talk over, around, and through me. On one occasion I was even climbed over! I might as well be invisible. Not from them a subtle, 'hello', 'good morning', or 'what have you been up to?'

Isn't there a course at teacher training college that covers the art of polite enquiry and good manners?

'I promise you, he said, 'hit it!'

Are you aware heat rises?

Well, it does and in my house if I was a spider living in the stairwell, I would be so hot I would be wearing shorts and a t-shirt, or shedding my skin. (Or do I mean a snake?) Be that as it may. You get the picture. The warmest place in my house is the staircase.

However, to moderate this airflow and meet it half-way, the original builders placed a radiator at the top of the stairs.

It's a bit like that song: *Something's gotta give. When an irresistible force such as you, meets an old immoveable object like me ...*

One lot of hot air charges up the stairs and on encountering a second lot of hot air, which stops it proceeding any further, stops dead, provided you keep doors exiting the landing closed.

Works like a treat. Only one snag ... If I want to be hot, I need to sit on the fourth stair and watch television through the mirror on the wall.

However, if I am happy to be cold or even freezing, I can loll about in a chair in the sitting room.

Then came the day when it didn't ... you know ... work like a treat.

Tragedy loomed large on the horizon as I discovered the radiator at the top of the stairs stone cold. So I fiddled, and twiddled, and diddled, and daddled, and on not achieving as much as a smidgeon of warmth called the plumber.

'Can't come today, I am booked right through.'

'But it's bitter cold and it looks like snow, and I'm pretty doddery.'

'Doddery?'

'Yes, you know, getting on.'

'Right!'

Silence while I was left to imagine lips pursing and head shaking. 'Well, as I told you, I can't come today.'

'So what do I do?' I wailed.

'Well ... er. You got a long piece of wood? Two by one, that'ud do it.'

'Probably,' I murmured cautiously.

'You know the bit where the pipe comes up out of the floor?'

'Er … yes,' I murmured, even more cautiously.

'Hit it! With the wood! Hard! If that doesn't work, I'll fit you in first-thing termorra.'

'Hit it! *You serious?*"

'Yes. Make it hard, mind.'

So I hit it. And guess what? It worked.

I suppose if I was awakened by a large piece of wood clanking my pipes, I'd start working pretty sharpish too.

Promotion, Promotion, Promotion

I'm supposed to be a writer and writers write – at least they did last time I looked. Tragically, I don't get time to write. In between phone calls from people insisting I have a problem with my router, (it used to be double glazing) and a mysterious female voice echoing 'goodbye' before vanishing into the ether, tweeting and blogging, deleting all the spam emails that people, with nothing to do and no place to do it in, spend their time creating ... and wishing somebody a happy birthday on Facebook, is it any wonder?

I'm sure Ernest Hemingway never had this problem. If I remember correctly, he swanned off to a new country, drank pots of the local vino, and dashed-off a book. The only thing I dash off is yet another email to my publisher asking what font they are using on the cover of *Kidnap*.

Isn't it about time we realised that we, the current inhabitants of this planet, are missing out big time on the best part of life? And no, it is not a sale at Harrods or John Lewis. It is tranquility.

When I was a kid in school we learned a poem by W
H Davies:

"What is life if, full of care,
We have no time to stand and stare.

No time to stand beneath the bows
And stare as long as sheep and cows.

No time to see, when woods we pass,
Where squirrels hide their nuts in grass.

No time to see, in broad day light,
Streams full of stars, like skies at night.

No time to turn at beauty's glance,
And watch her feet, how they can dance.

No time to wait till her mouth can
Enrich that smiles her eyes began.

A poor life this if, full of care,
We have no time to stand and stare."

Does anyone today ever do nothing, absolutely
nothing, except look about them? I wonder?

Answers on a postcard, please.

Aliens have landed

Remember those stories about UFO's? Doesn't it seem strange that since the turn of this century they have all disappeared? No longer do seriously intuitive people see their ships crisscrossing the sky at night like the tail-end of a comet.

If I was a believing man, I might, just might, say they've gone because they've completed their mission to infiltrate the human species.

Rubbish ... you reply.

Is it?

Next time you see teenagers hanging about in the street – take a good hard look. I suggest to you that most likely they are aliens in disguise. Nothing else can account for the ease with which they manipulate technology. Take my granddaughter. She walked into my house last Sunday and proceeded to grab a bunch of wires and connect my radio to my CD system (which, by the way, I've had for at least seven years without being able to use it), and get it working perfectly in two seconds flat.

Logic says that's not normal.

I'm normal.

My granddaughter has to be a supreme being ... in other words an alien. People like me can't possibly be alien; we are definitely earthbound humans.

'How can you possibly tell?' I hear you cry.

Well, for starters, normal people find day-to-day living a challenge. I would have needed at least a half-hour, plus specs, magnifying glass, instructions, dictionary, and a large glass of wine before I could have made my radio work.

My latest love affair

I have a new love in my life.
No, it's not a man … it's railways!

Okay, so perhaps railways and men share some similarities. Neither is totally dependable. Frequently they arrive late and the slightest bit of cold weather and they can't get started in the morning.

However, unlike men trains are rarely short tempered. Quite the contrary; train managers behave with great civility and cheerfulness. And trains go pretty much everywhere these days (except Somerset), whereas you often have trouble getting the man in your life to even go to the supermarket.

And can men introduce you to an amazing kaleidoscope of new people, new places and new scenery without complaint? You'd need to change your lover weekly to reap the changes in scenery that railways can offer. Usually with men it's same-o, same-o, and where's my dinner?

Yes, I know, Reading's a mess, bitterly cold with

nowhere to sit, and likely to stay that way for two more years. And the ladies' loo at Paddington resembles something from the stone-age, even though they have rebuilt the rest of the station.

Still, St Pancras is divine. It's an amazing feeling when, ticket in hand you arrive at the station and find your train waiting and ready to board.

You definitely can't do that with a man.

22 February 2012: Urgent message to passengers using Reading station

If you're standing on platform 7, please keep your eyes peeled. Arriving trains have developed a very nasty habit of leaving passengers behind.

Already the coldest station in Christendom, when the decision was made to completely rebuild it contractors, in their wisdom, instantly demolished all forms of shelter, even for guards and station staff. Now the station is dotted with people cowering behind pillars in an attempt to escape the bitter wind.

And that's when it happens.

Scheduled to have double-length platforms, when a short train pulls in at the lower end of the platform, the hovering, half-frozen, would-be passengers waiting at the upper end neither hear nor see it.

During my regular sojourns on Reading station while waiting for the train to Bath, I have witnessed any number of frantically gesticulating people sprinting helplessly

along the platform, in the forlorn hope that the driver of the train will see them and respond by taking his foot off the accelerator pedal. Except these days levers are most probably operated by hand. Same result though – a lot of left-over people screaming at the station manager.

Maybe it was dangerous in the old days when the guard kept his door open for you to jump in. Still, even that was preferable to another thirty minutes hiding from the wind while you wait for the next train, which you won't hear arrive unless you stand out on a freezing-cold platform.

Getting the priorities right!

We all know the world is changing but why do we always throw the baby out with the bathwater? There's loads of good stuff that has vanished from our lives which we should have kept.

Such as, I hear you ask?

Um … men standing up for women on the bus, and children giving their seat to someone elderly.

Saying 'good morning' instead of 'Alright?'

And replying: *'Fine, thank you'* rather than *'good'* if someone asks how you are.

And if cars are parked on your side of the road, remembering that oncoming traffic has priority. You don't just charge through with your eyes shut, wearing a belligerent and defiant expression on your face.

Still, things really have gone too far when McDonalds changes its recipe for milk shakes. They were the closest thing to heaven you could get. For ten minutes after your purchase, you were forced to wait, saliva dripping from the corners of your mouth, for the ice cream to melt sufficiently to slurp up through a straw. They were so divine, when I collected my daughter from hospital after her baby was born, we stopped at McDonalds for a Big Mac and a chocolate milk shake.

On Saturday, after a long day signing books at Waterstones in Canterbury, (It was fabulous if you're asking, *Running* and *Time Breaking* are super reads) I arrived at Paddington hot, thirsty and exhausted. 'Chocolate milk shake,' I said when I finally reached the front of the queue.

What did I receive? Chocolate powder carelessly mixed into mush!

How could they?

I stared in horror and took a cautious sip, my worst fears realised as my taste buds encountered a lump of the bitter, unmixed chocolate powder.

I mean, I'm happy to put up with horrendous weather, overcrowding on the tubes, delays on the railway and a lousy government … again.

But changing a life-saving milk shake?

Whatever are they thinking about?

What a crazy, mixed-up world

21 June 2012: Guardian Newspaper: Hospital doctors and GPs are taking industrial action on Thursday in protest at the government pushing through changes to their pensions …

25 Apr 2016: Telegraph Newspaper: This week's junior Doctors' strike lasts for two working days …

It wasn't like that when I was a girl.

Fifty years ago, if you phoned for a doctor they arrived, even at night. They were over-worked, under-paid but so, so caring. A doctor saved my life at three in the morning when I developed peritonitis. Sixteen years ago, a doctor met me at the cottage hospital in Wells in the middle of the night because my baby granddaughter had a temperature of +104.

Now they're going on strike! Whatever happened to the word vocation?

And, how come in this modern, technological, all-singing, all-dancing age you can't get an appointment with your GP?

Shall we consult our diaries? I can be ill in two weeks when I get back from holiday. That suit you, doctor? Good, shall we book it then?

And forget emergencies!

'I'm so sorry the doctor's emergency appointments are all booked up and so are his phone-calls. Please try later!

It's crazy, it's ridiculous, and it shouldn't happen. In 1916 maybe, but not in 2016.

Shame and the glitzy chocolate wrapper

The engineer arrived at my house early this morning to take away my washing machine which had developed a loud clank, interspersed with a worryingly discordant thud.

To unplug it, he had to delve into the cupboard and there he discovered my stash of chocolate. As he pulled it out one bar at a time, I watched it multiply into a mountain range the size of the Alps or Pyrenees (the hills in the UK aren't big enough).

Hastily I began an earnest prayer to some well-meaning deity asking if they would kindly shift time back to November. Then I might, in smiling and confident tones, explain that the chocolate was bought for the groups of small children who knock on my door at Halloween, chanting Trick or Treat. Then with dewy eyes and a change in tone remark, 'Sadly, this year, there were fewer than usual.'

That's when I remembered it was spring and with Christmas in between, it was unlikely he would have believed me, anyway.

'I'm a children's writer,' I finally elucidated, my red-faced gaze focussed on the brightly coloured packages. 'I get very stressed if a book isn't going well.'

The engineer gave me a funny look, then turned his eye away from the mound of, shall we say it, *"the stuff that lasts but a moment in your mouth and a lifetime on your hips."* No doubt he was thinking – she either writes a lot of books or spends every waking hour in a state of extreme stress.

Then he pulled out the washing machine.

Sixteen years' worth of frozen peas, peanuts, biscuit crumbs, and dried up raisins came with it, plus, a large handful of dead flies and spiders.

That's when I fervently wished a hole of substantial proportions would appear under my feet.

I could have died with mortification.

After he left, I became so stressed at being found delinquent in the housekeeping department that I drank several cups of coffee and scoffed half my stash, whilst washing the floor and removing the debris.

Then I was struck by the most awful thought.

What if he had actually counted the number of bars in the cupboard before he left with my broken machine? Maybe I'd better hurry out to the shops and replace them, in case, when he returns with my mended machine, he thinks I've eaten them.

A picture paints a thousand words

∞

Breaking news

Incident on the 8.43 from Bath to Paddington triggers general alarm

Nationwide hunt set in motion by First Great Western

I am standing on Bath station in the bitter cold of a Saturday morning, having already driven across a frozen tapestry of fields and ice-tipped tarmac. With the wind whistling down from Arctic shores, bringing with it blue faces and a clutch of chilblains, only the seagulls mocking us from the rooftops of platform 1 are happy with this weather, our shivering bodies desperately cuddling a take-away coffee in an attempt to keep warm.

Finally, a disembodied voice announces imminent relief for passengers on platform 2. Needless to say when the long, sinuous shape of the 8.43 eventually curves into view round a bend in the track, I am not the only one to show gratitude.

On the platform, a spontaneous chattering breaks out

as plans for the day hit the air, and even the seagulls raise their wings in applause. Tension then begins to mount as the sixty or so passengers, laden with bags and not a few children, begin a visual search of the slowly passing train looking for empty seats.

As a paid-up member of the union of rapidly aging persons (RAP), chivalry often invites me to ascend the train ahead of other passengers, and I sink into my allotted seat, greedily anticipating an hour of soporific pleasure.

Without warning, an alarm-call streaks through the train, the train manager's voice terse with stress and concern.

'Coach B is missing.'

Panic ensues, quickly spreading throughout the train, reaching down even to the platform where relatives wait, hands already raised in a farewell gesture. Every passenger concerned and involved except for those in first-class who remain inured in silence.

As the train departs, the guard repeats his message. The echoing words rebound across the empty space where the missing coach usually resides colliding headlong into passengers who are herding through corridors in search of their seats in Coach B.

It is nowhere to be found.

It is not on the train.

So where is it?

Overnight, Coach B has been kept under lock and key

at the Bristol terminus together with coaches A – H. How can it have escaped? The other seven are here, all brightly shining and tickety-boo.

The call is repeated every few minutes, my somnolent state abandoned in concern for the flailing bodies searching in vain for Coach B.

By now the hunt is fast becoming nationwide, with messages flashed by Morse code from station to station. Have you seen Coach B? If recognised do not approach, may be armed and dangerous. Call for back-up.

I can only wait and hope that Coach B has made it. And at this moment, as our train pulls into Reading station, Coach B is heading for the wild open spaces and a life free from servitude and drudgery.

Who can blame it?

Well – for starters, I guess the hundred or so people forced to stand between Swindon and Paddington.

Charity beginneth and endeth at home

I live in a terraced house that is less than 15 feet wide, with a garden some 33 feet long, and neighbours on both sides. People tell me all the time, 'your heating bills must be miniscule. You're so lucky.'

I used to be … because I had lovely stay-at-home neighbours. At least, they were on the one side. On the other were two lads who had never discovered the off-switch on their boiler.

Sadly, no more.

Unfortunately when the lads moved it was summer and, at the time, I didn't realise how essential they were for my continued well-being. Then winter struck. The bitterest winter for years and I was cold, unbelievably cold. Still ignorant as to why, I tried every bedroom in turn – rather like a demented princess without the pea.

(Or even with the pee because cold weather has a nasty habit of affecting my bladder, especially at night.)

As the wind changed so did I; first to the front bedroom then to the back, trying to keep warm. As I lay there teeth chattering and delirious with cold, I began to wonder if perhaps the UK had shifted northwards … and that the great cable anchoring us to the tectonic plates had been yanked free and repositioned a smidgeon north of the North Pole. But surely someone would have noticed?

That's when I worked it out. I needed cavity wall insulation.

About fifteen years ago when searching for a new home, I settled on where I am now because the houses were charmingly described as 'luxury build.' How was I to know they meant the sales brochure?

Okay, maybe I'm not the most observant person on the planet and it took me a couple of years to discover my bedroom door didn't close, and even longer to notice that the window closures on my rear window were a mixture of square and round edges, and the taps in the cloakroom were slightly different – at least they don't appear to match if I am gazing at them while sitting on the loo. (And please don't get me started on flat-head versus dome-head brass screws.)

Anyway, I bought the house, moved in, and my first action after I had had a cup of tea was to phone the carpenter to board over the loft.

Why your first task? I hear you ask.

Because … I once did an amazing Eddy the Eagle impression, which landed me in hospital rather than the bottom of a piste somewhere in Switzerland. I was in the attic of a previous home when, with the aid of an unsecured piece of polished board, which decided to upend itself, I travelled at speeds topping 90mph to the bedroom floor, via a large hole in the ceiling which I carved out during my descent.

Admittedly, the event did have its lighter side, when my six year-old daughter and her friend of a similar age arrived on the scene.

'Is she dead?' I faintly heard him ask.

'Oh, good, then I won't have to go to school,' was my daughter's reply.

Anyway, up I go to my newly boarded roof space to inspect the carpenter's work, which is when I discovered the house had no cavity wall insulation. All that existed between me and my neighbours (or do I mean my neighbours and me) was a sandwich of breeze blocks without the filling.

So, in this bitterest of winters, I sent for the specialists only to learn they cannot cavity-fill interior walls.

It was then suggested, by my carpenter who was touting for business, that I should line the party walls with sheets of ply. What a good idea, I thought, until I realised it would reduce the width of my home from a humble 15ft down to an even humbler 14ft 10ins.

Unfortunately, since both my front and rear walls are almost-all roof, filling the cavity has made little difference.

In truth, the only evidence of insulation is a large heap of black carbon balls which have found their way into the attic, both front and back.

The upside to this extravagance on my part is the colony of birds, mice and spiders that inhabit the eaves remain convinced they have entered paradise.

The downside is that while I am writing my stories, I am still freezing.

Which brings me back to my new neighbours, who, if you remember, haven't moved in yet.

When they do, I discover that lovely as they are they depart for work obscenely early and return even later.

If you remember from school physics, heat actually hates to sit and do nothing. Gregarious and a tourist at heart, it enjoys travelling to foreign climes where it mingles with the locals. In lay speak, this means that warm air from my property heads out through the breeze block wall into my neighbours' houses and doesn't stop until the temperature in all three properties has equalled out.

Ridiculous, I hear you cry.

Like to bet?

Unexpected daytime visitors will tell you that while I always offer a warm welcome, I also offer a decidedly chilly room (Around 60° F to be precise).

I might well be neighbourly and keep loud noises to a minimum, nevertheless, I have no intention of heating my neighbours' homes … they'll be asking me to do their washing next. And so, unless a visitor is scheduled to make an appearance, I leave the heat off during the day. Instead, I wear numerous layers and strap a hot water bottle to my chest.

At night when my prescribed dose of evening heat has been and gone and I am thinking of heading upstairs for an early night, lo and behold a miracle takes place … the temperature in my house begins to rise. On occasions it reaches the dizzy heights of 64°, exactly as if some benign god has come on night shift and switched the sun on.

Yep, the neighbours are in!

Christmas Day presented me with the best gift of all. The temperature inside my house soared to a magical 68°F (20° C in new money) because the neighbours on both sides were partying.

Government announce investigation into missing rolling stock

This is getting serious! Haven't First Great Western not yet cottoned on to the fact that on their mainline trains, there are supposed to be eight coaches. A – H: All identical.

First, it was Coach B that went missing. Yesterday, Coach C bit the dust. Same station, same line, same operating company, same day of the week – Saturday.

The only difference was the time of the train. An hour earlier: 7.43 not 8.43, as if the thieves are growing bolder. What will it be next Saturday – two coaches?

And guess what? My allocated seat was in Coach C.

Clutching coffee, two bags, and one of those tall display units that roll up inside a long, awkward tube weighing five kilos, I struggled for a seat, eventually collapsing into a spare seat in Coach B.

Where did the theft take place?

The train originated at Weston super Mare, less than

forty miles away. Was it held up by masked gunmen as it pulled out of the shed? Or stopped at a signal and disconnected by Starsky and Hutch or Sundance and his gang?

And why did no one notice this dastardly act?

Is this only the tip of the iceberg; the one we know about? What about all the coaches that go missing on other lines? Somewhere in the United Kingdom, is there a mastermind hell-bent on amassing hundreds of coaches?

I can only hazard the guess that this is a US-led plot, Machiavellian in its cleverness. The Americans have decided, without informing their British counterparts, that they are going to replace all those tatty-old tea sheds on wheels that lurk in laybys offering cooked breakfast, with smart diners made from our missing rolling stock.

Or, maybe First Great Western simply can't count to eight on a Saturday morning.

A shaggy dog's story

Authors always remember their first book. Sadly, dependent on whether it was a success or failure, the remembering is tinged with either misty-eyed fondness or total excruciating embarrassment that you could have written such drivel.

My first book *Scruffy* was a true story about my aunt's dog. A stray, with a most loving nature, he was deeply into mischief, hated vets and suitcases, and was a truly memorable character. I can't draw and having promised my family I would write about his adventures, invited schoolchildren to put pen to paper, with the most spectacular results. Originally sold to raise money for the Bristol Dogs' Home, Scruffy remains a firm favourite in schools even after ten years.

That's fantastic, I hear you say.

Well, it would be except, in the early years whenever I arrived at a primary school I was greeted by the cheerful words, *'Oh, it's the scruffy lady.'*

Note: Even when I was wearing my best clothes.

Bring back real bottoms

In this technological age, the ability to communicate with one's grandchildren presents an ever-increasing challenge particularly if you are hoping for something other than a monosyllabic response.

In my house, the usual result of any attempt at conversation is:

mobile phone 1: grandmother 0.

Nevertheless, it is imperative for the future well-being of grandparents everywhere that we maintain our position as the fount of all wisdom – despite not being able to run. No longer is it enough just to feed the 'little dears' and tuck them into bed at night, we also have to constantly reaffirm the dwindling belief, 'that we really do know best.'

Difficult, if not impossible, I hear you cry.

'Come on, we went to war for less.'

From long experience, I choose my battles, and the ground on which they are fought, very carefully and make sure the odds are stacked firmly in my favour before embarking on my campaign.

Unfortunately, since my daughter spread the totally unfounded, and quite malicious rumour, *never, never, never ask Baba a question unless you want a fifteen-minute answer*, any sort of skirmish has become something of an uphill battle. **In other words, I am scuppered before I start**.

Still, I am nothing if not a fighter, relegating skirmishes with my granddaughter to the car or walking down the street, when she can't run away.

And so it was one day, when we were strolling through Bath that I dispatched an opening salvo: 'As a matter of interest, what do you think about boys in pigmy-sized jeans?'

'What are you on about?'

'Trousers with a waist hanging off their buttocks and a crotch level with the knees.'

'Oh, those.'

'Surely, you don't approve. Not when you girls spend half your time drooling over film stars and footballers. Young guys who wear these sorts of trousers should be dragged into a clothes shop and forced to inspect their rears in a mirror.'

'Shush!' Granddaughter flashes an alarmed glance at passing pedestrians, *'Not so loud. Someone will hear.'*

'No matter,' I continue in a superior fashion. 'Besides permanently dislocating their knees … I mean have you watched how they walk? At best, it's somewhere between

70

a slurp and a shuffle. God help them if they ever come across a charging rhinoceros in the street that has escaped from London zoo.' (I throw in the last bit to check she is still listening.) 'Look what happened to James and the Giant Peach. James' parents were eaten up in no time.'

Snort of derision. *That's a story. Anyway, rhinos are vegetarian.'*

'You willing to test the theory?' I challenge bravely. 'Besides,' say I, warming to my theme, 'they look like they're wearing a nappy.'

Great – a muted giggle. Okay, firmly in the saddle of my hobby horse, I push my luck. 'And whatever do their girlfriends think? However besotted with the guy, no way can they consider baggy grey Y-fronts, on show for the world to see, an edifying sight this early in the morning.'

Hearing spluttered laughter, I decide my street cred as a grandmother has just been renewed (like my bus pass) for the next few months and wisely shut up.

Still, will someone please start a campaign to bring back real bottoms?

Whether the weather

What with Greenwich, the BBC meteorological unit, weather satellites, mediums, shepherds, red sky, clairvoyants and faith healers, how come you still cannot choose a dress for a wedding in a couple of weeks, and be certain of wearing it without being soaked to the skin, frozen to the marrow, or burned to a crisp?

Okay, so we are an island and most probably have the most diverse climate in the world, although I believe Melbourne, Australia, might run us pretty close. But not overtake ...

Still that's no excuse. I mean Tim Peake has just spent six months in the International Space Station. He could have phoned in each morning to give us an update on the weather for the British Isles. Especially since the space station was passing our front door every 91.63 minutes – give or take a second or two.

Surely, that's not too much to ask?

Everything comes to those who wait

Old English proverb, used, but probably not originated, by Violet Fane (1843-1905)

'Ah, all things come to those who wait, (I say these words to make me glad), But something answers soft and sad, 'They come, but often come too late.'

Rubbish!

Does this exclamation mark a disagreement with the ideas expressed in the poem or my intention to get rid of all the rubbish that has accumulated in my house over the course of a year?

Whichever!

It will happen and it won't be too late ...

How do I know? Exactly as I know every September swifts gather on telephone wires, chattering noisily, until, by some sense of intuition known only to them, they flock into the air heading for climes both warm and balmy.

As I stare at the spring cleaning tasks still waiting to be undertaken, I am neither shamefaced nor agonising about them. Were I younger, I would be fretting, disturbed by my inactivity, which goes against everything my mother ever taught me, and worrying myself into an early grave. My goodness it's April tomorrow, I must … I simply must begin. My goodness it's May tomorrow, I must … I simply must begin!

Fortunately, long experience assures me that it will happen … eventually … and therefore I am able to remain calm pursuing my daily routine of …

To be honest I am never quite sure what my daily routine consists of. Is it my morning cup of tea or the act of switching on my computer or even standing by the window admiring my garden?

So May, June, July; they come … they go. Still, I don't worry. It will happen.

And then comes the day which forecasters promise will be a scorcher … and definitely too hot to play golf. I head for the garden clutching a book and a coffee. After about half-an-hour the sun begins to sear my feet and my shoulders. Is it telling me something? Are its burning rays a reminder of things to come?

A thrill of excitement begins to work its way through

my body and I find myself full of calm intent. I head for the terrace which remains cool and shady no matter what the heat of the day and gather up a bowl of warm water …

… and start to wash the paintwork and windows inside and out.

After that, I wash the shower curtain, nets, and as the day clouds over and the heat lessens, return to the garden and clear out the shed.

Age and the antique sideboard

"We all know we have to grow old but no one said we had to be happy about it."

It is a generally accepted fact that old age cannot be appreciated by those for whom it still resembles some vague point in the future. For those of us who have reached that point, age is best described as owning an antique sideboard or an old-fashioned drainage system; still serviceable if treated gently but full of kinks.

Sadly, for those embarking on this era in life, new hurdles abound daily, and things you have once taken for granted begin to resemble an obstacle race. Climbing onto a stool to reach the top shelf of a cupboard requires giving your leg and knee muscles fifteen minutes' notice (at least it does with me, plus a lengthy debate as to which leg I should use). Compound this with a lack of spatial awareness, and stool-hopping becomes as complicated as heading out on army manoeuvres into the wilds of Borneo.

I mean, how many times a day do you hit your head because you have forgotten to close the cupboard door in the kitchen?

Me? I have ceased to count although recently my cranium has acquired some very weirdly shaped lumps and bumps.

As for my computer, this is now a minefield, full of booby-trapped spellings. Are there 2cs and 1s in necessary or vice versa? (And how the heck to you spell vice versa?) Is it definate or definite?

Once a touch-typist possessing skills beyond compare, these days my fingers blunder across the keyboard, typing 'ios' instead of 'ious' and 'o' instead of 'of', 'without' instead of 'within'.

Ah, such painful nostalgia remembering how my fingers flew across the keys.

'Focus on the positive, your garnered wisdom, your maturity,' is the advice of those who do not know what it's like to creak when you get out of bed.

The only good thing I can see to come out of old age is a loss of perfect vision and the need to wear spectacles to read.

'A blessing, really?'

Totally! Because now, whenever I glance at myself in

the mirror, unless I am wearing my glasses, which is a bad idea if I ever heard one, I can't see my wrinkles.

Now that's what I call a positive. Sometimes I even look youngish.

Note to self: Remember promise made to daughter to wear glasses when washing up, so I might actually see to rinse cups and saucepans clean.

Appearances can be deceptive

Fashion most extraordinary

I hate piercings. Ears I can tolerate unless there's a chasm in the lobe wide enough to carry the Gotthard Tunnel through the Swiss Alps. Even a neat stud in the side of the nose is okay until you go swimming when it most likely resembles the Trevi Fountain in Rome ... but tongues, lips, cheeks and eyebrows turns the wearer into an advertisement for *Edward Scissorhands*.

My daughter calls it, 'expressing yourself'.

My granddaughter just thinks I'm archaic. She actually likes *steam-punk*.

Now, let's be honest: how can piercing the septum with a ring that hangs down like fossilised snot ever be considered an elegant fashion accessory, except by primitives who lived ten thousand years ago? Such adornments should only be worn by something that has four legs, stands in a field, eats grass, and bellows a lot.

Okay, maybe you shouldn't judge a book by its cover

– but we do. We all do, *all* of the time! If a bloke sitting opposite me on the train is covered in piercings and tattoos, I make a judgement – and it's rarely complimentary.

Yes, I know that's prejudice, pure and simple. Still, we all have our pet peeves.

In my book, even if a guy is totally super, if he is all studd-ed up he has at best only a fifty percent chance of being recognised as such. And if he's wearing enough iron-ware to set-off alarm bells at Heathrow security, he'll never land a girlfriend … unless she's wearing enough iron-ware to set off alarm bells at Bristol airport.

In my book, people should be like that advertisement for Brita water: pure and simple, without additives.

Mr Heinz and I

Remember the years after the Second World War when food was in such short supply and the kindly, well-meaning people of Australia, Canada and South Africa sent us food parcels?

It was then as a small child I was introduced to tinned food: Epicure sausages, tinned peaches and condensed milk. (I once stole a small tin from the larder and tried to eat the evidence. I gave up a little way from the end.)

Food was so difficult to come by my mother exchanged sugar for tea, and housewives became a dab hand at spreading a loaf with butter and scraping it off again. And the Sunday joint always had a bone in it which ended up as soup on a Thursday.

My family were bombed out of Croydon and after the war I was sometimes taken to stay with our erstwhile neighbours who had been relocated to a tiny flat, five doors down from where Vera Lynn lived. Something that was pointed out to me every time we passed the house. *'That's where Vera Lynn lives. The forces sweetheart, you know.'* Sadly, I didn't understand the significance until I was grown up.

The little flat possessed a tiny corner cupboard in an equally tiny kitchen. Mostly empty, its middle shelf was the proud depository for two tins of Heinz Baked Beans, which sat awaiting my arrival. My introduction to heaven – beans on toast.

It was 'the thing', 'the tradition' that I had beans on toast for supper whenever I stayed with Mr and Mrs Noakes.

No one can estimate how strong childhood memories can be but I have stayed faithful to Heinz Baked Beans for 60 years. It didn't matter a jot that they stuck the price up and up till they reached 69p or 71p. My mother would turn in her grave at the thought of paying 14s 2d for a tin of beans; still I didn't care. They were Heinz and that was all that mattered.

I was about to celebrate our diamond jubilee (Mr Heinz and me) when he took out the salt, and turned nectar into tasteless pap! Heartless, odious man to trample all over my childhood dreams. I am now suing for divorce.

Okay, so I know the arguments about salt, and never use it in cooking (I mean come on, even the sell by date on my salt container has faded over time). Still, I can't help sympathising with the king in this nursery rhyme.

The King asked the Queen, and
The Queen asked the Dairymaid:
"Could we have some butter for
The Royal slice of bread?"
The Queen asked the Dairymaid,
The Dairymaid said, "Certainly,
I'll go and tell the cow now

Before she goes to bed"

The Dairymaid she curtsied,
And went and told the Alderney: "
Don't forget the butter for
The Royal slice of bread."
The Alderney said sleepily:
"You'd better tell His Majesty
That many people nowadays
Like marmalade instead."

The Dairymaid said, "Fancy!"
And went to Her Majesty.
She curtsied to the Queen, and
She turned a little red:
"Excuse me, Your Majesty,
For taking of the liberty,
But marmalade is tasty, if
It's very thickly spread."

The Queen said
"Oh!: And went to His Majesty:
"Talking of the butter for
The royal slice of bread,
Many people think that marmalade Is nicer.
Would you like to try a little
Marmalade
Instead?"

The King said, "Bother!"
And then he said, "Oh, deary me!"

The King sobbed, "Oh, deary me!"
And went back to bed.
"Nobody," He whimpered,
"Could call me a fussy man;
I only want a little bit
Of butter for my bread!"

The Queen said, "There, there!"
And went to the Dairymaid.
The Dairymaid
said, "There, there!"
And went to the shed.
The cow said, "There, there!
I didn't really mean it;
Here's milk for his porringer,
And butter for his bread.

"The Queen took The butter And brought it to His Majesty;
The King said, "Butter, eh?"
And bounced out of bed.
"Nobody," he said,
As he kissed her tenderly,
"Nobody," he said,
As he slid down the banisters,
"Nobody, My darling, could call me a fussy man – BUT
I do like a little bit of butter to my bread!"

Shame on you Mr Heinz – right your wrongs and restore your beans to their original fulsome flavour, then we might not need a divorce after all.

Buzzed by a very nosy bee

Isn't it wonderful, you might say, to be surrounded by school kids who are so eager to learn and so full of curiosity?

Well, you might, until you remember what happened to the cat.

I am good at my job, my sessions are fun, noisy, and very entertaining, and I leave the classroom to enthusiastic applause wearing a smile on my face. Except for the few occasions when I am not ... er ... wearing a smile on my face. Or if I am, my smile is neither wholehearted nor natural.

Why? I hear you ask.

Because very early on in my career, I learned that schoolchildren are hung up on age. (So am I)

They are also very bright.

They also hunt in packs ... like ravening wolves.

Has anyone a question, their teacher calls out?

I wait ...

'*How old are you?*'

Sidestep from me: Big smile. 'Very old.'

'How long have you been writing?'

Alarm bells sound and tension sets in: 'About fourteen years.'

A moment later: *'Did you always want to be a writer?'*

Big sigh of relief: 'No, I wanted to be a tap dancer.'

Laughter accompanied by second sigh of relief.

'How many books have you written?'

'Er, twelve.'

'How long does it take to write a book?'

Huge sigh of relief as I step back onto terra firma. 'About four months. If I begin in October I am usually putting the finishing touches by February.'

'Which is your favourite book?'

Diverted, my pulse begins to slow. I can see safety looming.

Then ... they go for the jugular.

'How old were you when you wrote your first book?'

At lunchtime, they are waiting for me in the corridor. I now know what a buffalo or bison feels like when it is singled out from the herd and surrounded by predators.

Their leader shouts triumphantly: *'We worked it out. One of your slides says New York 1973. That's over forty years ago!'*

At that precise moment the words toe-rag and killing enter my mind!

Almost a sticky end

I smelled gas last night. Immediately I scurried into the kitchen to check the burners, sniffing loudly.

No – nothing there, all off.

I went to bed and I smelled gas.

Diving down stairs, I went to check that I really had turned off the burners or perhaps it wasn't gas at all but another strange substance ... maybe fish (I'd had fish for supper).

I went back to bed and tried to settle and then my heart started pounding.

Is this the end? I thought, leaping out of bed ... again. *Will I wake up stiff as a corpse?*

Downstairs I ran, and into the kitchen ... sniff ... sniff ... sniff.

Perhaps it's the second sign of dementia, imagining smells where there are none?

So I checked.

The first sign of dementia is leaving the gas on.

The second sign is not noticing it's on.

So I went back to bed, not to sleep but to work out if there was a gas explosion which of my possessions I should rescue. That took me perhaps fifteen minutes of thought. Still, it was an interesting exercise, trying to decide what was valuable and what was not. Still unable to sleep, I climbed out of bed and peered out of the window, calculating if I would break my neck or just my leg jumping out. That's when I settled on what possessions to take: a duvet to break my fall and a memory stick.

Then I thought: that's rather a good position to be in – uncaring about material things. And with that happy thought I was just drifting off to sleep ... when I smelled gas ...

In bare feet and wearing only a nightdress, I tore out into the street sniffing as I went, and wonder of wonders my neighbour's bedroom light was still on.

'Can you smell gas?' I said, phoning him (and most likely waking him from a peaceful doze).

'Yes, it was me. I turned the wrong burner on. My gas bill will be enormous. It's all right though, this stuff won't kill you.'

Can you believe it?

My neighbour's one hell of a lot younger than me and cannot rely on the forgetfulness of old age as an excuse.

However, since it's common knowledge (both his and mine) that all his delicious cooking smells float straight through the kitchen wall into my house, wouldn't it be reasonable to assume his gas would too?

He may be a scientist who knows about such things as whether gas will kill you or not. Nevertheless, when I finally went to bed I left my window wide open … in case.

From the sublime to the ridiculous

In the early hours of Wednesday morning, after a neighbour reported seeing Barbara Spencer, the children's author, dive head-first into her rubbish bin minutes before council collectors emptied it, green-coated officials arrived at the front door of her residence in Somerset.

When they finally gained admittance, a very dehydrated and exhausted figure met them. Collapsed on the stairs and incoherently muttering, 'But they must be here somewhere', after several cups of strong coffee, the writer confessed she had spent the entire night scouring her house for two black memory sticks.

'Honestly, young man, it is one thing when Coach B escapes from your train, quite another when memory sticks – carrying all your lectures – vanish.'

'They have to be here somewhere,' she repeated, casting a despairing look around her house, in which chaos now reigned. Drawers dumped on the floors, clothes strewn round the room. 'I even checked the washing machine,' she wailed.

Promising that her dive into the tall green bin had been a last resort and would not be repeated, the author was left to get dressed and drive into town to replace the memory sticks by buying anew.

As the ambulance drew away from the kerb, cries of, 'My life is ruined. It will never be the same again. I'll have to move. Perhaps they'll come to light then,' echoed through the hush of this quiet residential area.

Note from Editor

It is my considered opinion that questions need to be asked in parliament about this catastrophic syndrome that consistently destroys lives; not only the lives of authors but normal people too. Had it been the collapse of a bank or building society, money would have already been set aside to compensate the multitude of innocent victims.

Surely, it's time for government to come clean and confess the secret that has been kept hidden from the general public for centuries: *The Borrowers* never was a work of fiction. They exist.

It seems these small creatures, despite every attempt to curb their numbers, are once again on the march. No longer content with removing a single sock from the washing machine, and the only working pen in the house, they are currently expanding their skill base to include a selection of more essential items such as spectacles, credit card receipts, car keys, earrings and pills. According to recent reports, they have been known to abscond with memory sticks, mobile phones and similar gadgets – such as those tiny squares of plastic that hold a grandchild's favourite computer game, and without which tears are a distinct possibility.

Later that week, I was lucky enough to interview the bereft and broken-hearted author. She confessed that these particular Borrowers must have been exceptionally agile to shin up the leg of her desk and remove the memory sticks from the drawer in which they had always lived.

'Maybe,' she smiled wanly, as we said goodbye at the door, 'they were trying to set a new record for a domino run and required two additional black rectangles to complete the picture. One can only hope and pray, they will return them once the record has been broken.'

I mean what other explanation is there?

Hoist with my own petard

Why is it always when visiting Canterbury enlightenment strikes? Back to piercings, I'm afraid. Whilst journeying on the local train service from London to Canterbury, a body consisting mostly of ironwork sat opposite me. Fair's fair, no signs of a disturbance. No pornographic literature or bottles of beer.

(Did I tell you about that time a group of football fans boarded the 7.43 am London train at Bath clutching carrier bags full of cans of beer? By the time the train reached Reading an hour later, one of the youths was in the overhead rack.)

Anyway, nothing so dramatic happened on this occasion.

So how did I become a victim of my own prejudice?

On arrival at Canterbury, in the politest and most educated of tones, the young man from the seat opposite asked if I would like some help with my suitcase up the steps! And down again!

Just shows … never judge a book by its cover.

Clean bowled!

As you have no doubt realised I am extremely sensitive about age. In that I take after my mother, who always maintained an age some six years less than the figure on her birth certificate, which was quite a surprise for life-long friends who, attending her funeral, discovered she was actually 89 not 84. And so reluctantly to deflect the inquisitive minds of my grandchildren, I told them I was 45.

To their credit, they didn't query the figure. And in the forties I stayed, eventually coming to a halt at 49.

Christmas for many families, mine included, means good china, sparkling wine glasses and a special festive cloth, with colour-coordinated napkins and crackers. In our household, the good china means Minton and Wedgewood, half-a-dozen plates, all different, which my mother bought from a pottery shop on the Hagley Road in Birmingham in the fifties.

Last week, on bringing them out from the cupboard, in which they reside the rest of the year, to wash them, I somewhat brashly and boastfully embarked on a long story as to how they had been acquired.

(Tragically, long meandering stories are frequently a product of increasing old age, accompanied by an entrenched belief that our childhood memories will prove as fascinating to our grandchildren as they remain for us.)

I related in detail how I always accompanied my mother to buy these plates and that we went by bus, not having a car.

I still recall the shop, glass-fronted with a centrally placed entrance, among a matching parade of shops that housed a hairdresser, where I had my hair cut.

I remember too, how she could only afford to buy one plate at a time, sorting through a cardboard box on the floor where they were stacked. Although hand-painted rejects they still cost ten shillings which was a huge sum when you received only £11 a week to feed and clothe a family of six. I can see her now, handing over a caramel-coloured note in exchange for her purchase, wrapped in newspaper.

The china plates delicate yet sturdy were all different. Stunningly beautiful, majestic even, one was banded with gold with a mouth-watering plum in shades of darkest burgundy in its centre; others bore flourishes of gold or green and grey in an explosion of skill and colour. As children we each had our favourite, jealously praying Mother wouldn't award that plate to someone else on Christmas Day. Mine had gold-tipped frills fired into the china.

Thoughtlessly, I continued my story with the words: 'That was in the fifties over sixty ...'

... and stopped dead.

My daughter looked at me and raised her eyebrows.

Then she and I fell into hysterics.

After a few minutes of, 'what's so funny,' an irate, yet perplexed-looking older granddaughter swept out of the kitchen, too naïve to realise that this spontaneous eruption of mirth was not the result of some obscure joke but an encounter with a mind-blowing mathematical problem: *How did a memory tracking back sixty years result in an age of forty-nine?*

Ten minutes or so later, she swept back into the kitchen to find us still howling with mirth. She left again bursting with righteous anger and high dudgeon.

She did eventually work it out but it took her a couple of years.

"Twould ring the bells of heaven, the wildest peal for years..." Barbara has found her memory sticks

(With apologies to Ralph Hodgson)

'*Where?*'

In my suitcase which I searched at least a dozen times.

Don't ask!

But you have to agree, it really is a tad suspicious. Just imagine if I had stayed in the rubbish bin – wouldn't I be regretting it now, out on the dump, cold and weary.

My mother believed, if your search is eventually rewarded the time spent looking isn't wasted. What rot! In the time I spent searching the house, tidying every single drawer in case, lifting the couch and the bed, pulling out the bookcase ... I could have written a best seller!

Seller! That reminds me, when I was looking for the missing memory sticks I didn't bother with the cellar. Reason told me since I never go down there, neither did the memory sticks!

A Family Tradition

It's that time of year when sentiment is hung on the Christmas tree in close proximity to the angel on its topmost branch. We sing carols while we are wrapping presents and whenever a youngster happens to cross our path, we tell tales of the olden days, never to be forgotten, when Christmases really were magical.

My Christmas starts early, with the arrival of my family to make the puddings; a tradition that dates back to my great-grandmother in the 19th century.

In the spirit of Christmas, I begin the festivities by imparting to my youngest granddaughter that Grandmother Cooke was in fact her Great Great Great Grandmother. Then after the weighing, measuring and mincing of fruit, all but the currants, the sieving of flour and the beating of eggs, the grating of nutmeg and the gentle touch of spices, we take it in turns to stir, all the time employing my brother's nose. Once he confirms that the mixture is up to scratch with the correct balance of spice and citrus, we each give it one last stir during which we make a wish and hope for it to come true.

Finally, having left the mixture overnight, I get up early the following morning to put the puddings on to boil. More time consuming than you can possibly imagine, out come the cotton cloths that are used every year. Boiled white again after use, they live in the airing cupboard while waiting for their annual outing. And I still use the same pan with a dent in the rim that my mother used. Too large for the modern family, that too lives in the back of a dark cupboard all year.

While waiting for the water to gently bubble, my thoughts fly back to other ancestors who have stood by a stove waiting as I am doing now.

My great grandmother, a regal woman of sufficient worth to merit a portrait in oils, in a dress of black bombazine, with a jet broach pinned to the shoulder; my grandmother her lisle stockings peeping out from under her almost ankle-length skirt, often baggy and wrinkled at the ankles. A pinafore was her badge of office, as was her glorious red hair tightly controlled in a bun. My own mother, often too tired on Christmas Day to eat her dinner, worn out from washing curtains and polishing brass; my sister who ran a restaurant and used the same recipe to enthrall customers at Christmas as had my great grandmother, which brought customers back in January to taste other culinary delights.

Then, for the past eighteen years … me, for my family.

Each one of us in our turn has waited, head bent to the saucepan, listening out for the tell-tale sound of bubbling that shows the water temperature has achieved perfection. Tied to the stove for the mandatory six hours of boiling, there is little to do except muse on the very different lives of the four generations and be grateful to be living in a century in which 'wickedly clean' is not considered proof of respectability.

I frequently check, hastening to refill the kettle when the water level drops. Even that is not the end. Clean cloths and two more hours on Christmas Day.

Although the recipe has never varied, over the years we have tinkered with non-essentials. The family is smaller and we have cut down on quantities. I no longer use silver coins, respecting the fragility of aging teeth, and I omit the libation of brandy which, when lit, flamed blue to thrill its waiting audience. However, there is still both custard and cream if wanted.

On Christmas Day after the traditions of turkey and trimmings, I bring in the pudding. And, as has happened each year for 140 years, there is an expectant hush that precedes the first mouthful. And an even longer hush afterwards, in which our palate dances a fandango of delight and our senses, overwhelmed with joyous satisfaction, soar to the heavens and refuse to return … until Boxing Day.

Grandmother Cooke's Christmas Pudding – dating from around 1850

2 lb mixed fruit large California raisins, ordinary raisins, sultanas, currants, candied peel (about 3 – 4 ozs)

6 ozs suet – beef

Loaf of white bread to make 6 ozs fresh breadcrumbs

2 ozs SR flour

7 ozs Demerara and Barbados sugar

Less than 1 tsp of mixed spice, nutmeg, cinnamon

About ¼ tsp salt

4 eggs

Juice and rind of 2 small lemons and 2 oranges

Milk to taste

Preparation

1. Weigh fruit and mince, except currants

2. Prepare breadcrumbs from loaf.
   Add rest of ingredients and stir thoroughly.

3. Cover with a clean tea cloth and leave for 24 hours.

4. Taste and adjust if necessary. You will find the mixture sweet on first stirring, the spices, lemon and orange take time to develop.

5. Allow family to stir and take a wish.

6. Add to your bowls. Cover with greaseproof, and a piece of sheeting. Use string to secure.

7. Tie sheeting in knot above bowl so you can safely lift it from the boiling water.

8. Add bowling water to saucepan, no further than halfway up the bowl. Bring to boil. Boil for 6 hours with the lowest possible heat – just enough to stir the water. Do not let water boil over or pan boil dry.

9. After 6 hours remove from heat, remove cloths. Run the edge of your knife across the pudding and taste. If you don't swoon – there is something wrong.

   Replace with clean cloths, greaseproof etc.

   On Christmas Day boil for another 2 hours.

(Modern day addition of tinfoil over the greaseproof can be used to stop steam running into the pudding)

Will happily keep in the deep freeze or fridge up to a year but not in the cupboard under the stairs because fruit flies will find it out … and celebrate Christmas early.

All that glitters is not gold

❧

While cowering in the dentist's chair

I spent the afternoon lying prone, first in the dentist's chair, then in the hygienist's chair – which wasn't nearly as comfortable and messed my hair.

It was an interesting exercise – one that sent me speeding home to smile in the mirror and then look for my calculator.

(More of that in a minute.)

The object of the session was to analyse what work needed to be done, and to compute its cost.

(Naturally, there were no travel brochures actually lurking in the dentist's office, although I am convinced, after taking a look in my mouth he would be planning a long summer cruise.)

I eventually became aware that something of a very serious nature was taking place in my mouth when the dentist, from behind his white mask, started spouting numbers followed by a series of sonorous *ums, ahs,* and *sorrowful sighs.* So alarming was the noise that I immediately, and somewhat surreptitiously, began to scan my bank balance on my mobile phone and apply for an overdraft, in the hope that if I handed over enough dosh, my dentist would deign to correct the problem. A problem, may I add, of which I was unaware until the dentist started *umming* and *ah-ing*.

At the end of the examination, there came the dreaded, very long, and even more expensive discussion about what could be done and about plaque.

For those unclear as to the meaning of the word plaque; plaque in the singular is the dirty brown stuff that supposedly clings to your teeth and sets up decay and gum rot.

Plaque in the plural are pretty little objet d'art, a bit kitsch, usually made of porcelain (there are cheaper versions made of pottery) which cling to the walls of your hall or sitting room rather than your teeth.

According to the list of numbers the dentist was calling out, I had got plenty of the former and none of the latter, since I hadn't visited Switzerland for ten years and Spain for about twenty.

Were you aware that eating food causes plaque that rots your teeth, inflames your gums, and costs a lot? I wasn't. My mother taught me that eating food is nice and incidentally keeps us alive.

Worse, its causes gum disease which leads to bone loss,

receding gums and loose teeth … which cost even more to put right. **Rather like the old lady that swallowed a fly – she got suckered in too**.

So, after careful consideration of my bank balance which tends to be devoid of zeros at the best of times, I agreed to visit the hygienist.

'Starches, you know carbohydrates, are worst,' I was told. *'Foods, like bananas, are worse even than sweets. You know food stuffs …* (long pause for a zzziz of her machine to quit zzziz-ing) *… that leave a coating on your teeth. And if you have to eat sweets, it is better to eat them all at once – and then clean your teeth.'*

Hey, hang on. I'm not having that. The whole point of sweets and chocolate, which I use in lavish quantities as an anti-depressant, is that they leave a yummy taste in your mouth. Besides which, provided I am regularly topped up with another piece of chocolate I am able to maintain an equable and friendly outlook. And you want me to go and clean my teeth?

'Then there's yogurt …'

Yogurt? Alarm bells begin to flash. (Or do I mean ring?) I waited while the hygienist moved round the chair to begin removing plaque (singular) from my top teeth.

'Yogurt is acid. Too much and it erodes the teeth – like drinking Coke all day.'

115

'Oh' I said feeling guilty about my morning banana and my evening pudding of yogurt, which I eat in the misguided belief they are doing me good.

'What foods don't cause plaque?' I said when I could open my mouth again.

'Protein. Tribes that only eat meat usually don't have any decay in their teeth.'

I waited some more.

'Of course, too much meat can cause bowel cancer, liver failure, and childhood rickets from lack of vegetables.'

Ah ha! I just knew there'd be a downside.

I waited and thought, listening to the plaque (singular again) tumble out of my mouth rather like an avalanche of rock in the Cairngorms.

'To sum up,' I said thoughtfully when she had finished. 'Eating food causes plaque, although these days we get gum disease rather than cavities because we all used fluoride when we were kids. However, the result is the same, and they are both equally as expensive to correct.'

'Well,' the hygienist blustered, *'Looking after your teeth is important.'*

So I went home and calculated a life-time's expenditure on teeth, then a lifetime of misery eating all the foods I detest simply to avoid creating plaque.

That decided me. A good set of dentures and you can eat what you like (you can even eat chocolate in bed) and banish going to the dentist forever.

Earth has frozen over – Official

Born into the generation that still believes banks are dedicated to the well-being of their customers (Okay, I believe in fairy tales too) and are the originators of the phrase, 'customer-service', I received rather a rude awakening the other day, when I went into my local branch of Barclays.

'I want to transfer some funds from my current account into my ISA,' I said. 'Here is the account number.'

'Sorry, I am unable to do that,' said the nice girl behind the counter.

'Why not?' I said.

'We no longer carry that service. You can take money out, though.'

'I don't want to take money out; I want to put money in.'

She shook her head. *'Sorry, we don't offer that service. I'm*

118

afraid we no longer manage these accounts in branch. You need to telephone our savings department. I can give you a phone number, if you like, and you can use our phone. Just dial 9 for an outside line.'

'I thought banks believed in security. Isn't over the counter more secure than a phone call?'

'Not really,' said the nice girl. 'You will be asked security questions in a phone call.'

(Are you beginning to get that sick feeling in the pit of your stomach … You know, the one you get when you go into a supermarket and find you can no longer identify from which bit of the animal your joint of beef or pork originates?)

I dialled the number.

An automated voice launched into a long-winded explanation of my 4 options … plus button 5 if you have forgotten what 1 − 4 were.

I press 1.

An automated voice launched into a long-winded explanation of my 4 options … plus button 5 if you have forgotten what 1 − 4 were.

Hastily, I press 2.

Great! A real live, living voice!

Gobbledegook and a mumbled name. But hey, that doesn't matter, I'm of an age when I don't remember names anyway. I identify myself with my full name and my account number. 'I want to make a deposit into my ISA,' I say.

'I need to ask you some questions. Your full name? Account number?'

I take a deep breath.

'Sort code?' the voice continues relentlessly. 'Address? Post code? Mother's maiden name? Date of Birth?'

'One-five, forty … er… er… Er … six,' I say.

'Age?'

Age! My grandchildren think I'm 45. I hastily crunch a few numbers on my calculator.

'64,' I say. (Oh! Come on – be reasonable. I didn't sign up for a maths exam when I opened my ISA.)

'Now some questions about your dependents.'

What! Questions about my dependents?

Haven't I made it clear that all I want to do is put *my* money into *my* account? What the hell do you need the name of my aunt, my uncle, and all 22 of my children for?

(You can see that I am becoming somewhat unhinged – quite normal after being forced to confess my real age.)

It was then I got this most horrific thought. What if I begin to suffer from senile dementia and can only remember the names of 21 of my 22 children? Is there an option to phone a friend or ask the audience?

And then I thought – I don't want this. I want a bank that I can walk into, who will handle all my business over the counter, face to face with a nice girl (or boy), who has my identity, plain as plain, in front of her.

So I said: 'I don't want this,' and put the phone down.

In the olden days (and they're not that old) the bank manager visited you in your place of business and sent you a card for Christmas, all because you had taken out a loan with them. Loyalty: that's what our generation believed in. Sadly, that's gone too.

I sighed. Perhaps it really is time for a change.

I walked down the street to a building society and went inside. 'If I open an account,' I said, 'can I handle all my business over the counter, face to face with a nice girl (or boy), who has my identity, plain as plain, in front of her?'

'*Yes,*' said the nice lady and produced a form.

A pleasurable outcome

What's on my mind? Not a great deal, the book is going badly. The plot has huge holes in it and at this rate I will be a hundred before it gets finished. On the bright side, I sowed a huge number of sharp sticks to stop the neighbourhood cats peeing in my garden.

Text to my daughter:

'It appears these days I am keeping a dog and barking myself.'

Inaudible groan … 'What's that supposed to mean, Mum?'

'You don't know?'

'I will if you tell me.'

'It's that postage stamp of a lawn at the top of my garden that I've been longing to get rid of. Finally, I grasped the nettle, or bit the bullet if you prefer, and got a guy to dig it up so I could have gravel.'

'Is this going to be one of your long lectures, Mum? I want to go out.'

'No,' I type in a dignified tone. 'And it's not a lecture. Anyhow, along comes this great guy who kindly warns me how heavy soil weighs, and manfully shifts the top six inches of turf and soil. Piling some in the garden bin, he dumps the remainder on the flagstones where I had already explained I wanted my garden seat.'

'*Go on,*' the letters appear on my screen.

'Announcing that since the garden bin is scheduled for collection the next day, and then not again for two weeks, he won't be returning to finish for at least three weeks, because for two of those weeks, he is holidaying in the Maldives, where he is hoping to swim and dive with manta rays, he departs.'

Anguished typing: '*No, Mum, please tell me you didn't?*'

'I did. By the time I had dragged the garden bin out onto the pavement – which nearly killed me it was so heavy – I figured I might as well have a go at shifting the rest of the soil. Two days later, my garden seat is installed and all that needs to be done is add the gravel.'

'*Oh! So that's what keeping a dog and barking yourself means?*'

'Yep!'

Big on exercise

I decided to give up the gym today. After all when you go up and downstairs as many times in a day as I do, you don't need an expensive running machine. All you need is a bad memory or a shortage of spectacles.

NO, THAT IS NOT A TYPOGRAPHICAL ERROR, I really did say bad memory or a shortage of spectacles.

Here's the thing: scientific fact: as you grow older your sight gets longer and your memory shorter. (Unfortunately, I can never remember if it is in direct proportion or indirect proportion) Anyway, I need glasses and because I work upstairs, I keep a pair upstairs and a pair downstairs.

Like all sensible people, I hear you say.

Totally! Until the day arrives when you find the pair upstairs missing.

You charge downstairs, scour the house and the car,

and then take up your downstairs pair. Five minutes later, you find your upstairs pair of specs where you left them, on top of the banisters.

So you charge downstairs to replace ... Okay, you get the picture.

Now, multiply that by a bad memory.

1 pair of glasses x 13 stairs x 15° = one very fit, but frustrated writer.

*15° equals the number of times on average I lose my glasses per day.

If you add my many other absentminded sorties, such as going downstairs to make coffee and then forgetting to take the cup back upstairs, or leaving my coffee cup upstairs when I want to make afresh, you will appreciate that saving money on health club fees makes good sense.

Then came the day when I had an operation on my tooth.

For that I had to take a course of antibiotics, gargle with a foul-tasting mouthwash to kill germs, use a special toothpaste, plus a different toothpaste containing concentrated fluoride (don't ask 'cos I don't know, I just paid the bill), with one of the two particularly soft toothbrushes with which I had been supplied.

The antibiotics didn't like me and started up a horrendous itching, for which I bought several tubes of special cream. Then the rain brought on a bad knee which meant rubbing in anti-inflammatory cream day and night.

Then, as an early birthday present, my daughter bought me several jars and tubes of very expensive face cream with which to restore my youthful bloom.

Full of sprightly ambition, I piled the entire caboodle neatly, side by side, on my bathroom shelf.

The crunch came when I found myself using mouthwash to clean my face! Too short-sighted to read the label, I only recognised it because it was deep turquoise rather than colourless.

Panic ensued. Now, a third pair of spectacles reposes on the bathroom shelf.

Okay, so pouring mouthwash onto cotton wool instead of witch hazel is not too serious. I can readily excuse that. Using anti-inflammatory cream instead of toothpaste to clean your teeth? That, dear reader is a different kettle of fish altogether!

Of course, having an additional pair of spectacles has not solved a thing. If anything, it's made life even more complicated because now I have three pairs to misplace.

"A rose by any other name would smell as sweet" (Romeo and Juliet)

The BT telephone directory is now but a shadow of its former self, thanks to the proliferation of mobile phones and the demise of surnames.

According to the Internet, the Dutch didn't think about surnames until after Napoleon had marched through their country, which seems an extraordinary statement. Did they consider the unpronounceable syllables of their language more likely to deter Napoleon's conquest than, say, cavalry and cannon?

On the other hand, we British have always believed in them. Like bread, surnames were the staple diet of this nation. Defining your class and status, they also kept people you disliked at bay.

Surnames were so essential to the success of your career, you could go through life knowing but never calling your boss by his first name.

(I refuse to be gender equal here because in the distant past few women rose to the dizzy heights of being the boss. Unless it was a shorthand and typing school.)

Of those dedicated to not rocking the boat, middle-class housewives were probably the worst offenders. Despite inhabiting the same street for thirty years, they still referred to the lady next door as Mrs … No first names here.

As for children! Horrors upon horrors! Our neighbours in Yardley were introduced as Mr and Mrs Stanley … and Mr and Mrs Stanley they stayed. And we stood up when a grown-up (as they were called then) entered the room.

In modern society, surnames have done a rapid nosedive into a ditch labelled 'equality'.

In any gathering where a hostess is over-seeing introductions of friends to other friends, the air reverberates with a chain-link fence of first names: this is Fred who's something in the city, Beth, she's a teacher; Jacob, Mary, Louis, Farouk, Heath and Jahinda, who I told you about at lunch last week.

Who?

With millions of Freds, Beths and Jacobs, we have toppled into a morass of anonymity.

Long gone are those heady days when a boy introduced to a likely-looking lass shared a dance, followed by a shy word or two. Wanting to see her again, he would sprint home and grab the telephone directory from a shelf in the hall. Then, clutching a cup of cocoa, he'd plough through it looking for a Smith or a Davis, maybe spelled Davies, who lived in Tunbridge Wells. Even better if, during their moment of conversation, she had confessed to living at home with her mum and dad, he might even be able to add an initial: Theodore, Thomas, Tommy or Tristan.

The following night, prefaced by a cough, he would then, with trembling hand and sweating brow, pick up the receiver and dial that hopeful number. 'Er, is Brenda in?' Pause. 'Er, you may not remember, we met at ...'

See what I am saying: Of course first names did have their proper place ... but only as an initial. It was surnames that identified who you were and from whence you came.

Today, if you aren't lucky enough to be awarded the mobile number of the girl you wish to see again, forget trying to track her down, unless you live in a country village of less than one-hundred souls. Searching for a Julie, a Cathy or a Brenda in a town or city ... you stand more chance of finding that elusive needle in a haystack!

According to the rules of baseball

With security uppermost in everyone's mind, staff in schools quite properly wear name tags bearing their surname and an initial: Miss F Jones, Mrs B Trinder.

They are called and indeed call each other, 'Miss Jones' and 'Mrs Trinder' whilst in school. Children also call out, 'Miss' or 'Miss Jones' or 'Mrs Trinder.'

When I arrive at reception, I am signed in and presented with a badge on a ribbon bearing the magical nomenclature: Visitor. Thus identified, and indeed identifiable, I am allowed to enter the sacred portals of the primary school, making my way to a classroom for the first session of the day.

'Children, this is Barbara,' their teacher calls out.

Strike 1

Or maybe: 'This is a very special guest, a real live author.' Turns to me. 'May they call you Barbara?'

Strike 2

131

'Come on guys! How about Miss Spencer in deference to my great age?'

Tragically, it doesn't work. It never works, even when I say, 'Well, I'd prefer to be called Miss Spencer.' No, the lure of the first name is relentless. All day long, it is *Barbara this* and *Barbara that*, with an occasional *Miss* thrown from some child new to the school, who hasn't yet learned better, which sets my heart rejoicing.

Then enter a male teacher. 'I am Mr Humphries.'

Strike 3

Of course you are a Mister, that's obvious. Looking like that, an Adonis in spectacles and beard, you simply cannot be a Miss or Mrs or even a Ms. How about, 'I am John Humphries or Fred Humphries or even Algernon Humphries?

Note to teacher training college: Please include in your syllabus a lecture on how to introduce yourself to colleagues and visitors to the school.

Paying homage to the literary world
Or
Bravery above and beyond the call of duty

I am sitting in the dentist's chair … Hey, do keep up. Scroll back to my earlier blog. I wasn't just making one visit.

This time, I happen to be musing on how crowded the Internet has become with book review sites. It is littered … No, littered is quite the wrong word; littered conveys a derogatory message. Festooned or adorned would be more appropriate. In my opinion, review sites are set up by the bravest of people who, in a past life, would have volunteered for a mission to introduce cannibals to vegetarianism.

Why on earth should you consider them to be brave? I hear you ask.

Because, instead of simply having an obsession with books and leaving it at that, they have taken it upon themselves to review them.

Ebooks read on a tablet, phone or Kindle now number

in their millions; some good, some great … and some totally dire. From the blurb and fancy cover, they may look great. And, indeed, they may not have any spelling mistakes, thanks to a spellchecker, but they lack even a basic knowledge of the writer's art. In other words, they are somewhat lacking in both style and plot construction.

Whoever it was that said, *everyone has a book inside them*, should have been shot at dawn. Everyone may well have a book inside them; still, that doesn't necessarily mean they can write one. Writing is a learned craft, as is tap dancing, hurdling and becoming an astronaut.

I mean you wouldn't undertake the hurdles in an Olympic event without a soupçon of training, now would you?

Besides which, it's bloody hard work.

No, not the writing. Everything else. One agent states on her website, "If you haven't spent as long editing as you have writing, don't bother to submit your manuscript." Another agent accepts or rejects a book on the first page.

And agents have it easy. They only have to read three chapters before they sense liberation and are able to head into a darkened room for a lie down.

Pity the poor reviewer! They have to be the toughest, bravest, most long-suffering race in the world. How do they do it? A bad synopsis, of which there are many, has me reeling and in need of a gin and tonic. A bad beginning and

I run screaming from the room. A series of bad chapters and I am likely to break the land-speed record in an effort to escape.

But these guys … these reviewers … on they go … page after page after page … all four hundred of them. Scott of the Antarctic had nothing on them. Stoically they wade through thigh-high drivel, flounder through chest-deep meanderings, and into trite, meaningless and banal conversation.

My advice to all would-be writers: if you can't afford a decent course, read children's books. Go to the children's section in the library and pick twelve novels at random from the shelves and read the first chapter of each one. Writers of children's books are usually masters. They have to be. One dull page and you lose your reader. So, Philip Pullman for sentence construction, Louis Sacher for magnificent story-telling, Anthony Horowitz for planning, Roald Dahl for fun, and Michael Morpurgo for everything else … to name only a few of the many authors I admire.

Yep! Reviewers are superheroes all right. Clutching a large brandy, I have no doubt they plough through verbose prose muttering, "It is a far, far better thing that I do now than I have ever done …"

By the time they reach the end, they definitely deserve their rest when they get it.

(Apologies to Mr Dickens.)

The winter solstice

December 21 should be deemed international brain day. This extraordinary product of evolution can sort red lights, green lights, blue lights, and yellow lights. Ambulance lights, police lights, fire-engine, and traffic lights. Christmas lights, headlights, dipped lights, and fog lights. Cats eyes, street names, shop signs, and roundabouts. Junctions, road works, speed bumps, and traffic calming. At the same time as listening to the radio, humming, deciding what to give your husband/partner/family for Christmas, mopping the windscreen, turning up the car heater, accelerating, braking, changing gear, and putting on the windscreen wipers.

Pretty good piece of kit, I'd say.

Rescued from the Slough of Despond

Just when you think the all-powerful mammon of commerce has finally managed to contaminate every citizen of the UK with greed and avarice, programming them to answer a 5am wake-up call in order to be first in the queue outside Next, Currys, Harrods or Debenhams, or indeed any of the temples to materialism that besmirch our fair land ...

... something quite wondrous happens

... the sun shines.

You drive out to the coast for a quiet walk by the sea and there you discover car parks as full as the beaches. Here, warmly clad people stride out in the sunshine accompanying their dogs, partners, children and even their grandparents for a walk along the beach, doing what people have done in this fair land since time immemorial ...

Go for a walk on Boxing Day!

God Bless 'Em!

Perhaps there is still hope the deadly virus sweeping our nation can be resisted. Maybe, out of its 65 million inhabitants, a few will remain immune to the ravages of modern society … mobile phones, computer games and shopping.

*Distance lends enchantment
to the view*

∞

A memory of childhood

As I watch my grandchildren stare at images burned into the acrylic surface of a DVD, the years crowd back to my own childhood. Maybe the two generations share little apart from the gift of self-absorption that life awards the young, allowing, for the most part, children to skate blithely through their early years, ignorant of the complexities of adulthood.

In my house, weekdays were confined to school, homework, and listening to the Archers, Goon Show or Dick Barton on the radio. Saturday meant golf for my father followed by a trip to the pictures.

Saturday morning frequently began with him cleaning his clubs on the kitchen table, pushing the breakfast cloth to one side – much to my mother's ill-concealed irritation – while he lovingly oiled the head and shaft of his woods. By the age of nine, if it was a nice day, I was allowed to accompany him to the municipal course, where, as a reward for dragging his trolley round nine holes, I was given a jam tart and a drink of Tizer.

Of the golf I remember little, apart from his swearing at people who possessed a squeaky trolley, who passed within earshot just as he was about to drive off, or his returning home with one of his clubs bent like a boomerang, beaten into submission after a bad hook or slice.

Then, it was Saturday night, my favourite part of the week when my father took me to the pictures, only me, although I had elder sisters; they mostly stayed at home with my mother.

Living in Yardley, we had at least five picture houses within easy reach; boasting names like: Tivoli, Regal and Sheldon. Two were within walking distance; the rest a short bus ride up or down the Coventry Road. We didn't have a car; my grown-up cousin who lived with us did. It was the first in the road, a brightly polished black vehicle with running boards, which attracted a permanent audience of admirers, both big and small, adults as intrigued by this new machine as we children.

And so we walked or took the bus across the border into fantasy land where the screens were lit by glowing Technicolor. On it, Cowboys and Indians fought pitched battles, and John Wayne vaulted onto his horse bellowing *Hi-Yaa,* a far cry from the ridiculous *walk on* modern film-makers are forced into using.

To my shame I haven't the slightest idea what films my father liked. In a world inhabited only by children, he was simply the obligatory adult who handed over one and nine for a ticket to the balcony, and provided sixpence for a vanilla tub of ice cream, while I feasted my eyes on the flashing images being played out on the screen.

If my memory serves, most of the buildings were of red brick. Only one in Kings Heath was white. With a façade like the prow of a ship, magnificent stained-glass windows loomed over the pavement tempting an audience to step inside, where white-marble steps with polished-brass handrails led up into a magnificent foyer. Here, a plush carpet, sadly rain-soaked and scuffed by the entrance, patterned in swirls of red and gold, beckoned you towards the dark grey of the sound-proofed doors. Such magical doors, opening up to let people out, they barred their faces to all and sundry unless you held a valid ticket.

Queues were the norm. People waited patiently behind a board on which were scrolled the words: *balcony queue here.* My father liked going upstairs – as did I. For a little girl the staircase was a magical gateway to fairyland, its gold-clad walls decorated with glittering candle lights, its shallow treads perfect for floating up and down in imitation of Ginger Rogers or Rita Hayworth.

From minute to minute, the appearance of the commissionaire elicited an immediate frisson of excitement. 'Two,' he would intone, holding up two fingers. Conversation ceased as the crowd awoke, those at the back poking people ahead of them, encouraging them to step forward, as if rushing forwards would immediately empty further seats. Someone hissing, 'Go on, that means you.'

The foyer was dominated by black and white photographs of famous film stars, their faces as well-known as your own, and certainly as often seen. Far grander than any of our celebrities today, every word fed to the public was carefully scripted to enhance the magic that was cinema.

Tickets, small with the consistency of blotting paper, slid out from silver-coloured slots. If you were heading for the stalls, you were given only a moment or two to savour their texture and colour, just long enough to cross the carpeted space, where an usherette snatched them from you and ripped them in half.

Whether you sat upstairs or down, the moment the doors open you were captivated. Like a moth drawn towards a candle flame, the screen grabbed you with its bright images, stealing your attention away from the task in hand, that of negotiating your way to your seat through intense darkness, guided only by the downward spiral of an usherette's torch.

Yes, of course, it would have been more sensible to keep your eyes on the torch beam – but who could? It was as if your eyes, your entire being, was glued to the screen. The moment you entered that darkened space, your head flicked towards the glorious images playing on the screen … and didn't look away again. Sometimes mistiming the width of a step, you stumbled over its white edges and twisted your ankle, the pain swept away by the recklessness of a pirate, who was swinging athletically through a forest of rigging.

'Excuse me!'

Seats banged up as people, clutching umbrellas, trilbies and raincoats to their bosom, their eyes never wavering, fixed straight ahead, levered themselves upright, so you could reach your allotted seat. And, after an obligatory second, scarcely long enough to stuff your coat under your seat, you joined them – mesmerized by the story playing out on the screen.

I only once remember seeing an organ, a massive chord announcing its appearance, rising up out of the ground in front of the stage before launching into a light-hearted medley of popular dance tunes. As lights dimmed for the start of the film, with a final triumphant blast it descended below ground again, leaving usherettes with torches to guide latecomers to their seats.

On rare occasions, my route to the screen was blocked by a hat, for ladies wore hats back then, and I'd be forced to perch on the back of the seat or my father changed places with me. Often the film broke down, leaving black squiggles on the screen accompanied by laggard speech, and a fluttering noise as the broken film flapped loosely against its metal spindle. Groans and coughs filling the auditorium, plus the obligatory piercing whistle, rapidly changed to cheers as the projector whirled once more into action.

'Do we have to?' I'd mutter, when the film reached the point at which we'd come in. Dragging my feet, my head still fixed to the screen, I'd reluctantly squeeze my way past

147

those still happily watching. Sometimes, we'd accompany the crowd out at the end and, if hungry, call in at the chip shop.

Soaked in salt and vinegar and wrapped in newspaper even their taste is embedded in my memory. I don't remember how much they cost. 'Six-pennerth of chips' sounds familiar. In Small Heath, where Smith's Crisps was located, outside the gates they sold bags of broken crisps for a penny.

In all the years my father and I went to the cinema, I never once wondered why it was usually only the two of us. And it was not till years later that I learned my father hated being at home and my mother hated him being there.

I wish I still believed in that gentle deity whose job it is to protect children from the heart-wrenching lives of adults, at least long enough for them to learn how to cope. I never did understand why my mother or sisters couldn't be bothered to listen when I prattled on about the tap-dancing feet of Fred Astaire, or the tenor voice of Mario Lanza, or the swash-buckling sword-play of Stewart Granger – unless I was guilty by association.

Life goes down to the wire

Back in the wars between the cousins Red and White, Richard III purportedly cried, 'A horse, a horse, my kingdom for a horse,' as in the middle of battle his barons deserted for Henry Tudor, and his horse was cut down from under him.

You will note in the last sentence the word horse is repeated four times. For that is how important the animal was to the past; both as a measure of wealth, and as the method of transportation, a horse being an up-market alternative to a donkey.

Tragically, its eventual decline was heralded by the introduction of the internal combustion engine, and its use as a war horse in a cavalry regiment by the war of 1914, when even generals eventually came to the conclusion that galloping hooves were no match for machine guns. Now the noble beast, shorn of its accoutrements, either flies over hedges or dances round an arena to music.

Nevertheless, will anything ever be as wondrous as the horse?

As the instrument that took life cantering through the pages of history, it has lasted thousands of years. Can anything else endure this long?

Concord certainly didn't!

So why this musing in praise of a horse?

Am I now going to extol the virtues of the internal combustion or jet engine?

No, I am about to focus the remaining words of this blog on the existence of a small piece of wire. Not any piece of wire … a long, thin piece of wire with a plug on one end, without which civilisation, as we know it today, would fail and come crashing down.

… the humble charger.

On the train yesterday a young woman, before disposing of her luggage, whipped out this 'never – leave – home – without' item searching for a socket, and changed her seat three times before she found a functioning unit. (She had mistakenly entered the quiet carriage.)

Buses, trains, anything that moves, now feel obliged to offer both charging and WiFi points …

Does the success of business and life itself now depend on this?

Waiting for a train at the wondrously rebuilt Birmingham New Street Station, I found the platform awash with stylish fingers skimming over keyboards and loud-voiced conversations in which the intimate details of Aunty Minnie's sex life were shouted into a mobile, presumably to some interested party at the other end. Business deals worth millions of dollars were also being touted on that same platform while I, spoilsport that I am, stood in my little bubble of silence ... and thought longingly of ... er ... er ... silence, I guess.

And all of this is down to a single piece of wire.

If Shakespeare were alive right now, he would doubtless alter those words of Richard III to: *A charger, a charger, my kingdom for a charger.*

All good things come to he who waits

✎

153

Alan – A Singular Man

In all honesty it should be John the Jazz telling this story except he is too busy networking. A typical showman he is driven to wooing every female in sight – regardless of age or beauty – as a buttress for his own fading charms. Quite harmless, of course, this dalliance carried on in plain sight; John has no intention of landing himself in trouble with the hotel owners for flirting. Tall, white haired, bronzed and rounded of body, he is still handsome, although I expect he has crossed the three score years and ten barrier. He eulogizes about his legs, more, I suspect, as a crowd pleaser than anything else.

'Maria?' he calls out to the maid across a sunlit courtyard.

She pauses and leans on her broom, always happy to take a break from the daily routine of cleaning dozens of apartments for untidy and sloppy tourists.

John the Jazz hauls up the leg of his shorts – to a respectable height, for John is never offensive: 'See these legs – they're still good – the rest kaput.'

155

Maria, from Bulgaria, short and dark, and about thirty years his junior, laughs and calls out a few flattering words in broken English.

I recall a gossipy snippet about Joan Collins. 'Of course the legs are the last to go.' Sadly, I acknowledge that in my case they were the first.

So it has fallen upon my shoulders to tell the story, while John continues to bring filtered rays of sunlight into the lives of young and old sitting round the pool, and I berate myself, for the umpteenth time, for being so stupid as to go away on holiday on my own.

For me, holidays are always the same, a period of time that has to be endured; so why do I persist in putting myself through it? Hotels cater for couples. A single person – correction a single female person – is an anomaly. No one quite knows what to do with her.

This year, I chide myself, it will be different. Therefore, immediately on arrival, I pluck up courage and trespass on to the hallowed ground of the swimming pool, where a scattering of silent sun-worshipping bodies can be seen.

Among them are two vast ladies, deeply absorbed in their novels, who belong to that group of amorphous humans that never move while the sun remains overhead. Their radar is so finely tuned it can pinpoint the exact millisecond the May sunshine leaves the orbit of their gargantuan flesh. In a flash, they leap from their chairs and re-arrange themselves and their recliners into a new position, aimed at maximum exposure.

Then there's the obligatory retired couple, who are first into breakfast and first to the pool, where they remain all day but never swim. Also a slightly younger pairing neatly attired in matching shirts, shorts and hats, deeply attentive to their matching books, who recline at the same angle – one knee bent up – beneath the shade of a large umbrella.

There is also a bored young woman tending the pool bar.

The silence is overwhelming and I retreat to my room for a sleep – always a good option.

I feel obliged to explain that I am not of the generation that arrives at a hotel, leaps straight on to the diving board and shouts to the world at large, 'Hey I'm here. Anyone wanting a good time, shout Ay!'

No, I am of the generation of English women who know their place: quite willing for a gentle 'good morning' to suffice for the first day; to be followed up by, 'what wonderful weather,' on the second, only evolving into full-blown conversation and sparkling repartee on day seven … one hour before departure.

Nevertheless, I could write a book about how unfriendly couples, studiously rubbing suntan lotion into each other, can be. Most believe a woman who travels on her own to be a pariah, a freak of nature, someone to be feared. Even a stilted 'good morning' in her direction might prove fatal. Convinced that one unwise word and they will find themselves listening to an out-pouring of a lifetime of illnesses, they can't imagine anything worse.

Indeed, to be fair, is there anything worse?

There just might be. An unwary, 'Oh, tomorrow, we're going on the Heraklion tour, aren't we John,' might elicit a, *'That sounds wonderful. May I join you?'*

And how do you get out of that?

So like canine submission, I need to prove to the world at large that I do not suffer from verbal diarrhoea and have no desire to latch on to someone else's holiday plans. I do this by sitting quietly under my umbrella for an entire day, stirring only when some sudden poolside activity breaks my concentration. At which point I glance up with an intelligent and amused smile, aware that I remain a figure of deep suspicion as long as I remain reasonably presentable and don't look half-bad in a swimming costume.

Sadly, mistrust and suspicion are often among the many objects we pack in our suitcase to take on holiday. Buried deep in the recesses of the human psyche, particularly the female psyche, primeval urges quickly manifest themselves.

(What is it about wall-to-wall sunshine, umbrellas and loungers?)

While mistrust of foreigners is endemic like Aedes Egypti, the mosquito, so is a general mistrust of interlopers, especially the female variety, who is regarded as someone likely to be on the prowl.

Rubbish, I hear as cries of objection rise plaintive into the air.

Trust me, a few days lounging round the pool, and nights sipping a glutinous concoction of obscure alcoholic beverages, and strange things begin to happen to the libido of even the most placid of husbands. And so a wife, plagued by mistrust and suspicion, dare not speak to a lone female, in case it stirs her 'usually docile' husband into flirtation mode, and a husband daren't speak, in case his wife thinks it.

Was it not Noel Coward who so vividly described the midday sun and Englishmen?

Strangely enough this barrier rarely applies to men travelling on their own. A spare man is like manna from heaven. Wives welcome them with open arms considering them an unexpected bonus, a hint of spice in an otherwise boring meal. And husbands? They are pretty well acquainted with their wife's libido after thirty years of marriage, and are not the slightest bit bothered by a harmless flirtation. Besides, after three days round the pool they are in desperate need of some sensible conversation about football or fishing.

The following morning, once again armed with a determination to make this holiday something other than bloody awful, I attend the travel rep's welcome meeting, where the rest of yesterday's intake are gathered.

A pathetic sight, no wonder the rep plies us with drink. Most you will never see again, except on the coach taking you back to the airport. Instantly forgettable with white legs and arms, new holiday clothes and wearing an 'easily pleased' antenna, they are busily signing up for every excursion going. There are also the obligatory complainers, severe-looking couples who are determined to make their displeasure felt to anyone who will listen, because thus far the holiday does not resemble the brochure in the slightest.

And there is a trio of men travelling alone.

The youngest of them is very young, very pale, and very serious, with glasses and long, neatly pressed grey shorts. There is no way he will attract covetous glances from the opposite sex. The best he can aim for is to awaken some long-dormant maternal feeling in the bosom of one of the more elderly ladies scattered round the pool.

The second is a direct contrast. Overly large and wearing flamboyant patchwork shorts, his shirt fails miserably in its attempt to restrain the yard of flesh protruding windward. It takes no time at all for him to tell all those unfortunate enough to be within range, that he is here to lose weight. He could be okay. He knows about football.

… And then there is Alan.

It is impossible to decide what hits you first. The chin? Spiked with greying stubble, it protrudes way beyond the rest of his face. Or the electric blue Lycra shorts and shirt, presided over by a black cap? His clothes identify him as a dropout from the Tour de France and he is carrying a fold-up bicycle to boot. This has been damaged in transit and is being reported to the holiday rep. He is also somewhat bent, with a serious chest deformity on which your gaze immediately becomes fixated; a misshapen bulge running from waist to shoulder that pushes out his skin-tight Lycra top. It's almost as if, the surgeon treating him for a humped back has effectively cured it by popping the bulge to the anterior with a sledgehammer.

That evening after surviving my second day by the poolside, with a gentle and elegant dip when no one is looking, I am dispatched to the far end of the beach for dinner, where the hotel owner's brother has a restaurant.

If you look at an agency contract closely, it usually stipulates that bed, breakfast and evening meal will be provided. It says nothing about eating in the same hotel as you sleep.

The restaurant is empty except for two people, the youngster and the somewhat florid gentleman, whose face after a day in the sun now rivals his shorts. Remembering my determination to enjoy this holiday, I ask politely if I might join them.

If I am asked, 'What is the single most important event of that year?' I will readily confess it was taking that first step across the restaurant floor, although at the time I was consumed by misgivings.

The youngster turns out to be sensible, knowledgeable, and possessed of those earnestly dependable qualities that appeal only to bank managers in a society based on credit bashing, binge drinking and clubbing. Ten years down the line he just might come into his own, when blond bimbos, having experienced an army of good-looking wasters finally accept that they do not make good life-time partners, and begin their search for something more stable.

The large florid gentleman, in the vast pink shorts, is either a paranoid schizophrenic, who regularly forgets to take his medication, or he suffers from an over-active imagination. With conspiracy theories to end all conspiracy theories, from Mrs Thatcher and British Telecom taking over the world, to a Thai doctor who injects wealthy business men with AIDS in order to steal their money, talking to him is like a mystery tour – you are never quite sure where his sentences might end up. Exhausting; especially when he comes out with such gems as, 'I was travelling on Rumanian Airways and there was a draught.'

Very much later I return to my room to sleep, thankful I have not eaten dinner alone, although dreading my week in such company.

The following afternoon after the duo return from their day's excursion, it is a matter of simple courtesy to stroll around the pool and say hello. That is when Alan appears, clad in his day's Lycra offering of black and purple. Perching on the edge of the recliner, he says little, not really joining in, more waiting for someone to notice him.

It is awkward and in vehemently denying any suggestion of snobbishness, I would like to say in my defence, that Lycra on a retiree is not really something a delicately brought-up lady wants to mix with!

Then John the Jazz arrives.

He has spent the day working the crowd around the pool and is now in need of a fresh audience to bewitch and bedazzle. Before long he is regaling some outrageous part of his history. Without warning he stops, his aging memory refusing to recall a name.

'Is it ...?' says Alan quietly.

It is.

John swings round and for the first time registers the curious figure including him in the circle he is busily entertaining.

Then conversation becoming more general turns to football. A question pops up, to do with a Chelsea player from a bygone era.

'Is it ...?' asks Alan humbly.

It is.

We stare as John succumbs to a mock apoplectic fit. Wild horses wouldn't drag me away from that circle now. I peer at Alan closely. Beyond the Lycra and the chin are a pair of brilliant blue eyes through which he squints, a set of perfectly even white teeth, and a masterly brain.

By the time our hilarious session reluctantly draws to

a close, it has become clear to every one sitting there, that if you want to know anything you ask Alan.

'Who played in the 1970 FA Cup Final?'

'What was the name of that film star who murdered his wife, and got off?'

'The President of Albania?'

'The beginnings of Jazz in London?'

John the Jazz, upstaged, reacts like the typical showman he is, producing mock-spluttering rage and mimed neck-wringing. All in all, there is so much merriment the poolside residents raise their collective heads from their books in shock.

From that point on, the holiday takes off like a rocket heading into space. During the day we go our separate ways but from late afternoon, like bees around a honey pot, we gather round Alan, and exactly like flowers, we blossom. On our last night we all go out to dinner, including several of the poolside couples, who have come to the conclusion we are having way more fun than they are.

Not the gargantuan ladies, however, of whom one is a vicar. Sadly, I had come to the reluctant conclusion that she is progressing up the same avenue as the large florid gentleman. According to her, she was preparing her sermon one night in her study at the seminary and felt someone sitting behind her. Turning round she saw Jesus and said to him, something like, 'These are your words,

Lord, you should read them not me.'

At a loss for a response, only later did I think up what I should have said. 'Why on earth didn't you ask Christ to step through the door and meet a few of your colleagues, thus settling the debate once and for all?'

Maybe I am prejudiced against the cloth. Seems fair. After all, she spent an entire evening bending my ear about her progress through religion and then two days later, when I spoke to her in the swimming pool, pretended to be Greta Garbo.

'I want to be alone,' she gasps theatrically. 'This is my holiday and people won't leave me alone.'

'I only asked when you go back to work?' I protest.

At *our-last-night-of-the-holiday-dinner*, couples sit together for security. Feeling myself in distinct danger of being propositioned by our hostess, I plonk myself down next to Alan who, in honour of the occasion has substituted his Lycra for an old pair of trousers and a fisherman's jersey.

John the Jazz, of course, sits in regal splendour on his other side. Quicker on the uptake than me, he has already sussed out that in Alan (whom he insists on calling Reg, after Reg Harris, World Champion sprint cyclist in the fifties) he has discovered something unique. I totally agreed after spending several hours in his company walking along a precipitous mountain path to view a monastery. He had joined us at dinner one evening earlier in the week, (me and the young geek, who I hasten to say has turned out to be the most delightful and charming young man. Perhaps it was his shorts that were at fault). During our meal I learned that he rationed himself to ten Euros a day. He ate breakfast and something relatively cheap, like spaghetti Bolognese, for dinner.

And it is at dinner this last evening I discover, to my great relief, that his deformity is caused by an overly large money-belt purchased in the local market for a few euros.

On the far side of the table sits our resident paranoid schizophrenic, whose stomach has by this time reached the two-yard line, over which buttons and button holes refuse to leap. Relatively normal in the full light of day, as the sun sinks towards the horizon he deteriorates rapidly, and is now regaling those seated around him about the Zionist / MI6 plot to eliminate him, and stop him whistle-blowing on the government. Already they have bugged his television. Having sat through the story several times, I just know his audience is in for a roller-coaster ride.

Alan undoubtedly is by far the safer option.

Born in Kent and a union man, he admitted to being a firebrand as a youngster. In sober middle age, this has turned to calm disgust at the corruption of modern government – particularly the one he championed for so long. Married, divorced, his family has pretty-much disowned him. I expect it was the Lycra which was bestowed on him as a job lot some ten years earlier, when he was living in unbelievably straightened circumstances. Obsessed with a determination to travel, he has taken to wearing Lycra instead of holiday clothes. Washed at night – hung up to dry – no ironing needed. Perfect for a man living on £45 a week.

This came about because the Job Centre, in their wisdom, decided a man couldn't possibly live on £45 a week, his wage from his part-time job. And so they offered him six weeks full-time employment, with no guarantee of anything afterwards. Now Alan liked his job as a cleaner at a local college, and he was happy. It had taken him a couple of years to find even that, and without an iron-clad guarantee of employment after six weeks, he quite logically refused – rightly preferring the bird in hand.

Concluding that anyone this obdurate had to have money stashed away, the Job Centre cut his entitlement to benefit. Alan didn't argue but set about living on what he earned.

It was John the Jazz who told me that Alan never burned heat, only in the severest of winters. Instead, he rolled himself in a blanket, stuffing a hot water bottle between him and the blanket. He never used the emersion either, boiling a kettle for hot water. Breakfast consisted of oatmeal porridge (buying large sacks cheaply), sweetened with a little wild honey. And for dinner, pilchards in tomato sauce were stirred into potato (you know those huge tins that cost 40p which are frequently fed to non-fussy cats). Once a week he visited (and still does) the supermarket, filling his trolley with whatever is out of date, bent or damaged, all the goods he can lay his hands on for a tenner.

And for entertainment he listened to Radio 4.

Finally, after ten years he was granted a pension of just over £100 a week. For him this was a fortune. He made himself live off £60 because somewhere amongst all this high finance he was still paying back a debt to a Holiday Club. In the wildness of youth, he had fallen victim to a scam and signed an agreement to pay £5,000 for which he would get free holidays in Spain every year. He never got the holidays but still had to pay the five grand. The rest he spent on going places. Constantly checking for last minute deals – no matter where – he packs his Lycra and bicycle and off he goes.

I wish George Bernard Shaw could have been one of our party around that dinner table. I would have backed Alan against Alfred P. Doolittle any day, and after talking with him, no doubt the great man would have agreed.

We parted next day. Most are returning home after a week's holiday. Only Alan and John the Jazz are staying longer, John explaining that he is thinking of marrying Maria and settling down.

'I haven't got many years,' he explains. 'For me, the sunshine, wine and the affection of a good woman will be like getting to heaven early.'

Swearing to keep in touch by email there are murmurs of a repeat visit next year. Except it would never work. It was the thrill of discovery which gelled such a disparate group, and this element in any future encounter will be lacking.

Still I confess to a hankering to find out what is in store for Alan. He is the type to *'have gone over the top'* in the First World War, despite his abhorrence for war. I just know he will be junketing around Europe until he is too old to move. And then quietly, without any fuss, he will die.

So please, if a man in Lycra, with piercing blue eyes and greying stubble decorating an overly large chin, turns up in your holiday destination, say 'hello' to him for me.

Songs and Poetry used in this book

Books by Barbara Spencer

Broken

Kidnap

An Audio version of *Kidnap* is also available

Time Breaking

Deadly Pursuit: 2 book series. *Running* and *Turning Point*

For Children

A Serious Case of Chicken-itis

Scruffy

A Fishy Tail

The Jack Burnside Adventures: A Dangerous Game, The Bird Children, The Lions of Trafalgar

Legend of the Five Javean

The Amazing Brain of O C Longbotham